Code Of Canon Law

Canon 66 «The Christian economy, therefore, since it is the new and definitive Covenant, will never pass away; and no new public revelation is to be expected before the glorious manifestation of our Lord Jesus Christ.» Yet even if Revelation is already complete, it has not been made completely explicit; it remains for Christian faith gradually to grasp its full significance over the course of the centuries.

Canon 67 Throughout the ages, there have been so-called «private» revelations, some of which have been recognized by the authority of the Church. They do not belong, however, to the deposit of faith. It is not their role to improve or complete Christ's definitive Revelation, but to help live more fully by it in a certain period of history. Guided by the Magisterium of the Church, the sensus fidelium knows how to discern and welcome in these revelations whatever constitutes an authentic call of Christ or his saints to the Church.

Christian faith cannot accept «revelations» that claim to surpass or correct the Revelation of which Christ is the fulfilment, as is the case in certain non-Christian religions and also in certain recent sects which base themselves on such «revelations.»

Maria Valtorta:

The following are selected chapters from the notebooks of Maria Valtorta, the Visionary credited with having the greatest impact in our understanding of the Gospels since the Apostles in that she was the recipient of a series of private revelations (1943-1951) directly from Our Triune God and various other Blessed souls including the Virgin Mother, The Apostles John and Paul, Saint Joseph, the Angel Azariah and Many others.

At age 28, Maria Valtorta offered herself as victim soul and for 36 years, she bore untold bodily and spiritual suffering on behalf of her fellow man. She died on October 12th 1961, aged 64 and was buried in Varreggio, Italy. With Ecclesiastic permission, her remains were moved to the Basilica della Santissima Annunziata de Firene in Florence, in the chapel of the Grand Cloister

These 'novelettes' are selections of the dictations by subject, for easier study, with minor editions to remove directive commentary that was not part of the original vision or dictation and, where necessary, also grammatical editing to smooth translation errors, without altering or interpreting in any way, the content received in the visions and dictations themselves, except perhaps unknowingly through translation errors. Bearing in mind that these visions and dictations are meant to address issues that have plagued mankind from the beginning of time, and are as relevant today as they will be millennia from now and until the end of time, the foot notes, to foster understanding, attempt to anchor various points within the texts in the context of the events taking place in the world at the time the dictations took place.

Don Dolindo Ruotolo, Priest:

Father Dolindo Ruotolo, born in Naples, October 6th 1882, the eve of the feast of the Virgin of the Holy Rosary – died, in Naples November 19th 1070; Italian Catholic priest, Franciscan Tertiary and venerated as a Servant of God by the Catholic Church. .» Considered by many to be a master of Neapolitan spirituality in the Catholic Church, he was laid to rest in the Church of 'San Giuseppe dei Nudi'. The cause for his canonization is presently in course.

Even in life he was famed for his holiness. Padre Pio of Pietrelcina is known to have said of him to the pilgrims from Naples: «Why do you come here, if you have Don Dolindo in Naples? Go to him, he's a saint!»

Dolindo was a scribe and a mouthpiece for the Holy Spirit, knowledge and Wisdom infused from above, a Capuchin Friar miracle worker of no lesser significance than Padre Pio of Pietrelcina,, stigmatized in Christ's name, an honoured son of the Virgin, who was initiated to the knowledge and the Wisdom of the scriptures, a faithful servant who wanted to be humbled before Christ and above all an agent of God amidst the people.

While sill a young man he rested his gaze on the Virgin's image and pondered on the unbalance between the duty he had undertaken and his natural talents, which were not so bright. He felt unworthy and so as a young candidate for the great office of priesthood, he turned to his Heavenly Mother and prayed in his heart: «if it is your wish that I become a priest of God, let the treasures of knowledge flow into my mind and in virtue ensure that I become worthy». A placid sleep then fell on the brow of the devoted child in prayer, and through sleep the

Holy Mother instilled in him the seven gifts of the Holy Spirit.

He used them from the moment he awakened until the end as keys for his internal harmonium and sung with all his heart praise to the Trinity and Mary. His knowledge shone not for vainglory of human science but for the dignity of the divine

illustration of the foundation of the Catholic faith towards which flows each and every path of human doctrine.

Jesus and the Virgin visited him with intimate consolation and to exemplify his election they gave him crosses to bear, crosses of incomprehension by both his family and his parish, crosses of expiation for his brother's sins, crosses of redemption for the salvation of God's flocks, who came to him night and day sent by their Shepherd to be purified of leprosy of the heart and diseases of the soul.

He bore upon himself, in the likeness of Christ, the weight of the cross for all men, and little by little as he climbed with Jesus until Golgotha he felt his shoulders sag and his spine bend under the burden of the cross, his legs stiff from the difficult journey bleeding with disregard to the bandages. It felt like the fatigue of age and yet it was the stigma of Christ ever patient, a weary soul until the final hour.

The Full of Grace:
The Early Years.
The Merit.
Joseph's Passion.
The Blue Angel.
The Boyhood of Jesus.

Follow Me:
Treasure with 7 Names
Where there are Thorns, there also will be roses
For Love that Perseveres
The Apostolic College
The Decalogue

The Chronicles of Jesus & Judas Iscariot:
I See You As You Are
Those who are Marked
Jesus Weeps

Lazarus:
That Beautiful Blonde
Flowers of Bounty

Claudia Procula:
Do You Love the Nazarene?
The Caprice of Court Morals

Christian Tenets:
On Reincarnation

Christian Tenets

Lamb Books
Illustrated adaptations for the whole family

LAMB BOOKS
Published by Lamb Books, 2 Dalkeith Court, 45 Vincent Street, London SW1P 4HH;

UK, USA, FR, IT, SP, PT, DE

www.lambbooks.org

First published by Lamb Books 2013
This edition
011

Text copyright @ Lamb Books Nominee, 2013

Illustrations copyright @ Lamb Books, 2013
The moral right of the author and illustrator has been asserted
All rights reserved

The author and publisher are grateful to the Centro Editoriale Valtoriano in Italy for Permission to quote from the Poem of the Man- God by Maria Valtorta, by Valtorta Publishing

Set in Bookman Old Style R

Printed and bound by CPI Group (UK) Ltd, Croydon, CR0, 4YY

Except in the USA, this book is sold subject to the condition that it shall not, by way of trade or otherwise, be lent, resold, hired out, or otherwise circulated without the publisher's prior consent in any form of binding or cover other than that in which it is published and without a similar condition including this condition being imposed on the subsequent purchaser

Christian Tenets:

On Reincarnation

LAMBBOOKS

Acknowledgements

The material in this book is primarily adapted from 'Notebooks 1944' and 'Notebooks 1943' By Maria Valtorta, 'Mystic and Visionary, Inspired Writer - nick named, Little John, after St John, the Evangelist- of 'The Poem Of The Man God (The Gospel As Revealed To Me), first approved by Pope Pius XII in 1948, when in a meeting on February 26th 1948, witnessed by three other priests, he ordered the three priest present to «Publish this work as it is», With excerpts from 'Who Dies Shall See' by Don Dolindo Ruotolo, Priest, 1882-1070.

In 1994, the Vatican heeded to the calls of Christians worldwide and have begun to examine the case for the Canonization of Maria Valtorta (Little John).

The contents of these Notebooks do much to clarify the sublime nature of religion and go a long way to answering questions that have plagued humanity for centuries at least, if not all the way back to the beginning of Time.

Mystical revelations have long been the province of priests and the religious. Now, they are accessible to all. May all who read this adaptation, find it edifying. And through this light, may Faith be renewed.

Special Thanks to the Centro Editoriale Valtortiano in Italy for permission to quote from Maria Valtorta's work.

Christian Tenets

Contents

January 7th 1944: Jesus.	14
The Intercession Of The Souls In Purgatory	17
January 9th 1944: The Eternal Father.	21
January 9th 1944: Jesus.	26
January 10th 1944: The Spirit Of God.	30
January 10th 1944: Mary.	34
January 10th 1944: Maria Valtorta's Witness:	37
January 11th 1944: John.	45
January 11th 1944: The Apostle Paul.	50
January 17th 1944: Jesus.	55
May 25th 1944: Maria Valtorta's Witness.	65
May 25th 1944: Jesus. In the Evening	74
June 29th 1944: Jesus.	76
The Soul In Purgatory Of Montefalco	80
October 08th 1943: Final Repentance And Saving Mercy.	90
October 09th 1943: The Continuity Of Life In God. 1 a.m.	92
October 09th 1943: The Common Destiny And Special Service.	95

January 7th 1944: Jesus.

Jesus Says:

«**M**an, who are dear to Me, in spite of your errors, lost sheep for whom I have walked and for whom I have shed my Blood to point out to you the way of Truth, this dictation is for you; An instruction for you. Do not refuse my gift.

Do not commit the sacrilege of thinking that another word is more rightful than this one. This one is Mine. It is My voice, which for centuries has always been the same, which does not change, which does not contradict itself, which is not renewed with the passing of the ages because it is perfect, and progress does not affect it. You can update yourselves. Not I, who Am as on the first day in My doctrine, just as from eternity I Am forever in My nature. I Am the Word of God, the Wisdom of the Father.

In My one, true Gospel it is stated: 'I Am the God of Abraham, the God of Isaac, the God of Jacob. Not the God of the dead, but of the living.[1]'

Abraham lived once. Isaac lived once. Jacob lived once. You shall live once. I, who am God, took on flesh once

---

1   Matthew 22:32

and will not take it on a second time, for God, too, respects order. And the order of human life is this:

For a spirit to be fused to flesh to make man like God, who is not flesh, but spirit, not animal, but supernatural. For the flesh, when it declines, in its evening, to fall like a slough and covering into the nothingness from which it was taken and the spirit to return to its life-blessed, if it lived; damned, if it Perished for having made the flesh its lord instead of making God the lord of its spirit.

For that spirit-from the hereafter, whose details you uselessly wish to know, without contenting yourselves with believing in its existence-to wait, with a fearful trembling or a joyful thrill, to see the flesh rise again to clothe itself therein once again on Earth's last day and to plunge with it into the abyss or penetrate into Heaven, also glorified in matter, with which you have overcome because it has been your natural enemy, changed into a supernatural ally by you.»

But how could you take on one flesh at the time of my sublime review and go to condemnation or glory with it if each spirit had many fleshly existences? And which would it choose from among them? The first or the last?

If the first was valid, according to your theories, for the spirit's accession to the second, it is already meritorious flesh-indeed, more meritorious than the others to possess heaven, for what exacts an effort is the first victory. After the accession, it is protracted. But if only the perfect are to enter Heaven, how can the first flesh enter? It would be unjust to exclude the first and unjust to believe that there will be exclusion of the last one of your fleshly existences, which, by an infelicitous theory, you believe can clothe your spirit-like a suit laid down in the evening and taken up again in the morning-embodied and disembodied and embodied once again, in an ascending series.

And how could you invoke the blessed if they were already reincarnated? And how could you call your deceased yours if at that moment they were already the children of others?

No. The spirit lives. Once created, it is never destroyed. It lives in Life if it has lived on earth, in the only life which is granted to you as a child of God. It lives in Death if it has lived in earthly life as a child of Satan. What belongs to God returns to God forever. What belongs to Satan returns to Satan forever.

And do not say, 'This is bad.' This-I, the Truth, Am telling you-is supremely good. If you lived a thousand lives, you would become Satan's bait a thousand times, and you would not always be able to emerge wounded, but alive. In living a single time and knowing that your destiny resides in that time, if you are no t accursed worshippers of the Beast, you act at least with that minimum of will which suffices for Me to save you.

Moreover, blessed are those who, instead of the minimum, give their whole selves and live in my Law. The God of the living observes them from Heaven with infinite love, and the good you still have on earth is had through these saints, whom you sometimes disdain, but whom the Saints call 'brothers and sisters,' whom the angels caress, and whom the Triune God blesses.»

The Intercession Of The Souls In Purgatory

Extract from 'Who Dies Shall See...'
By Dolindo Ruotolo, Priest. Ch XIII

There are numberless examples of graces, some miraculous, obtained through the intercession of the souls in Purgatory. We can say that their care for our soul and our body is such, because they know by experience what damages a soul. Thus in their suffering they have a greater and loving pity for our suffering. They were also once pilgrims on earth, they know the dangers for the souls and what people suffer in their body. Being in a state of perfect charity, the souls in Purgatory, when they receive suffrages from someone on earth, feel the responsibility to help him much more and in a better way, because they have a greater feeling of compassion for him. For these reasons the souls in Purgatory not only pray with more efficacy for those who offer suffrages for them but, with the permission of God, they sometimes intervene personally in our sufferings and our dangers.

In 1649 a famous librarian of Cologne, William Freyssen, made a vow to distribute one hundred books on the souls in Purgatory in order to motivate the faithful to offer suffrages for them. Shortly after that, his son and his wife both gravely ill and close to death, were restored to health. (Puteus Defunct, book V, art.9).

In Paris in 1817 a poor maid, well educated in the Christian life, had the pious habit to have a Requiem Mass celebrated every month, notwithstanding her meagre income, for the souls in Purgatory. She actually would be present at the holy Sacrifice, uniting her prayer to those of the celebrant Priest, to obtain a better deliverance for the soul in most need. One day she fell ill and had to go to the hospital. Since she could no longer work, she lost her job and was then unable to satisfy her pious habit for lack of money. When she left the hospital she was left but with a few cents. So she recommended herself to the Lord to take care of her and began looking for another position. Passing by a Church, she realized that it was the day that she usually would have a Mass offered for the souls in Purgatory. She presented her little money and asked to have a Mass celebrated. During the Holy Mass she prayed fervently for the souls in Purgatory and for Divine Providence not to abandon her. Then tired and anxious, she continued to go to from place to place in search of work. Walking towards her along the street, a young nobleman, well dressed and very pale, stopped her and said:

«You are looking for a maid's job, am I right?»

«Yes, Milord» she answered, surprised.

«Very well, then go to this address. There is a lady there that will give you the job.» And then he disappeared in the crowded street, without even giving her the time to thank him.

The good woman immediately went to the address the young man had given her and as she was going up the staircase to the house, a maid was coming down, very upset, with a bundle under her arm. She asked her whether the lady of the house was at home and the woman rudely told her to go and ask the lady herself, when she opened the door because as for her she was leaving for good. The woman knocked at the door and a noble lady came to open it. The woman told her what had happened to her and asked if she needed a maid. The lady was very surprised because she had just fired her maid a few minutes before due to her poor manners. She wanted to hear again what had happened and the woman repeated her story, looking around the room. On the mantelpiece she saw a picture and she said:

«Here he is, madam, you have the picture of the young man who sent me here and gave me your address.»

On hearing this, the lady gave out a shout and lost her senses. When she recovered, she hugged the woman with joy and said:

«My dear, from now on I shall consider you as my most dear daughter and not a servant. My son died two years ago and it was because of the Mass you had celebrated that he finally left Purgatory. May the Lord be praised. Stay with me and work in my house. We shall pray together for the souls in Purgatory that the Lord may deliver them soon and may enter the blessed Homeland of Paradise.»

We did careful research on this story as well as on many other cases that attest to the protection of the souls in Purgatory for those from whom they receive suffrages.

How great is their help for our bodily needs and how much they care for our spiritual wellbeing! The results of their protection are not as visible as their protection in our physical needs, but how many good inspirations, holy thoughts, victory over temptations, miraculous conversions at the point of death are due to the fervent prayers of the souls in Purgatory for those from whom they received benefits.

How marvelous is the Communion of the Saints! What a marvelous view, says the Count De Maistre, it is to see an immense city of souls with their three orders in relation with each other with no interruption: the world militant is united to the suffering world holding tight to the triumphant world!

January 9th 1944: The Eternal Father.

The Eternal Father Says[2]:

«I continue to speak to you, man, and to all those who, like you, are worshippers of deceitful idols.

There is no need to have an Olympus, like the pagans in ancient times, to be idolaters. There is no need to have fetishes, like the savage tribes to be idolaters. You, too, are idolaters and with the most opprobrious idolatry, you that adore what is not true, that serve a religion which is nothing but the worship of Satan, that adore the One in Darkness because you do not want to bow your perverted heads and even more perverted hearts before what was guidance and supernatural light for millions and millions of men who were also among the great of the Earth- and with the true greatness of the mind and the heart- who in this supernatural light and guidance found the lever for their elevation, the comfort of their lives and the joy of their eternity and to whom the world, in spite of its ongoing evolution, looks with admiration, regretting the fact that it no longer has in itself that faith which made those great ones great on Earth and beyond the Earth.

Since the marrow of your souls is not nourished with

---

2   I thought it was Jesus speaking but it is he Eternal Father.

true Faith and the knowledge of those eternal Truths, which are the life of the spirit, you that have committed the crime against yourselves of denying the spirit created by God, knowledge of the Law and the Doctrine given by God and call Religion superstition and describe its forms as useless, regard yourselves as superior even to those great ones, who, in your view, should not be absolved of the sin of diminishing themselves to the level of a silly ignorant woman in having shown devotion to the Church and obedience to Religion, which is nothing but the substance of my Law and the Doctrine of my Son- true worship, therefore, of a true God whose manifestations are undeniable and certain. All of them: from Sinai to Calvary, from the Tomb crushed by Divine power to the thousands and thousands of miracles which, over the course of the centuries, have written God's glories and the truth of his Being in time, as words of fire which does not fade out, of molten gold which is not obscured.

And like madmen tossing splendid jewels into the sea and carefully gathering pebbles, or rejecting healthy foods in order to fill their mouths with filth, in exchange for the Religion of God, which you reject, not finding it worthy of yourselves-pseudo-supermen with Satanized minds, corrupt hearts, and prostituted spirits, idols, in turn, with feet of clay[3]- in the place of the Religion rejected, you then accept the demoniac worship of the Enemy of God and become his ministers and proselytes*.

These are the critics of My religion; these are the judges of My Church; these are the accusers of My ministers; these are the indicters of My faithful! They see My religion; the Church, priests, and the faithful, as an object of mockery and a source of degradation. Then

3   **Daniel 2, 31-36.**

they, who say man doesn't need religion, doesn't need
priests, and doesn't need ceremonies to respond to God,
make themselves a dark, occult religion, laden with
a whole secret rite that bears no comparison to the
straightforward, light-filled rite of My religion. Men as
corrupt as they are, or more so, become its ministers,
in whom they believe with blind faith, and they take
the histrionics** of these men, possessed by Satan, to
be the voices and manifestations of God. They become
proselytes- and how observant they are!- of this obscene
parody of worship, of this sacrilegious lie.

*A person who has converted from one religion to another

** Excessively theatrical

Here they are. Here are the ones who, in the place of the
holy God, of the eternal Saviour, set the Entity and the
hellish entities, and they bow down to the ground before
them- these, who regard it as unworthy of a man to bow
before a true altar upon which My Glory triumphs and
the Mercy of My Son shines and the vivifying Love of the
Spirit flows, and Life and Grace come out of a Tabernacle
and a Confessional, not because a man- like unto you in
matter, but rendered a repository of a divine power by the
Priesthood- gives you a little host of unleavened bread
and pronounces for you a formula of human words, but
because that bit of bread is My Son, Living and True, as
He is in Heaven at My Right Hand, with His Body and
Blood, Soul, and Divinity, and those words make His
Blood rain down- which is pained over having poured
out for so many of you, sacrilegious scorners of It- as it

rained down from the height of His Cross, to which My love for you had nailed Him.

But do you not reflect, O speudo-supermen made of putrid slime ennobled by no light, on your inconsistency? You reject God and worship the idols of an obscene, demoniac religion. You say you venerate and believe in Christ and then flee from His Catholic, Apostolic, Roman Church; you set a cross in the place where you call the Enemy of the Cross and of the holy Crucified One. It is as if you were spitting the regurgitation of your interior upon that Cross.

And what greatness do you see in your farcical priests?

In the mass of mine there are many who are deserving of reproach. But what about yours? Which of yours is 'holy'? The best ones are lustful, gluttons, deceitful, and proud; the worst are crooked and savage. But among yours you have nothing better. Nor could you have anything, for if they were honest, chaste, sincere, mortified, and humble, they would be 'saints'- that is, children of God- and Satan could not possess them to lead them astray and lead you astray through them.

After years and years in which they term themselves 'instruments' in the hands of God, have they improved their nature? No. Such as they were, so they remain - if they don't actually get worse. But don't you know that contact with God is a continuous metamorphosis making a man into an angel? What good advice- later confirmed by facts- have they ever given you? None.

They say one thing to one person and another to another

on the same topic, for they are Satan's bait and I, I the Supreme Power, confuse their ideas of darkness with the unbearable splendor of my Light, which they cannot endure.

That Light is joy and guidance only for My children, who soar into the future times with it in their hearts, not by their own power, but by its power, and with the eyes of their spirits see and with the ears of their spirits hear that which is God's secret, the future of man, and in My name say what the Spirit places upon their lips, cleansed by love and made holy by pain.

Diviners, astrologers, savants and doctors of the Satanism, which My Son condemns and which I cover with a twofold condemnation, with a threefold condemnation- for your Satanic religion, which camouflages itself in pompous names, but is nothing but Satanism, is a sin against Me, the Lord of Heaven and Earth, before whom there is no other God, is an offense to the Son, the Saviour of man, ruined by Satan, and is an offense to the Holy Spirit, by your negation of the known Truth- realize that I turn your occult science into foolishness and prepare the sternness of an eternal future for you, that have not wanted Heaven as your kingdom and have wanted Satan, not God, as your pontiff, king, and father.»

January 9th 1944: Jesus.

Jesus Then Says To Me:

«   aria, you have offered yourself unreservedly, haven't you?[4] You want souls to be saved through your sacrifice, don't you?
And then don't you consider that I told you[5] that souls are conquered with the same weapon with which they are lost? A soul's impurity, with purity, Pride, with humility. Selfishness, with charity, Atheism and luke-warmness, with faith. And despair, and despair, and despair, Maria, with your moments of anguish which nevertheless do not despair, but call God, look at God, seek God, and hope in God, even when Satan, the world, men, and events seem to conspire against hope and ally themselves to say, 'God does not exist [6]'

In this Satanic hour you are living through, whereas only

---

4   Act of offering as a victim to Divine Justice and Love delivered Friday, June 12, 1931, feast of the Sacred Heart of Jesus. She herself recounts his approach in his autobiography and in a catechesis on 10 February 1946, page 182. It is at this time that Jesus revealed to Sister Faustina and asked him to generalize the devotion to the Divine Mercy (February 22, 1931)

5   On July 18, 1943 in «The notebooks. 1943 «

6   Psalm 14 (Vulgate: 13); Psalm 53 (Vulgate: 52)

one weapon should be used to overcome Satan's war on God's creatures, whereas it would suffice to invoke My Name with intrepid, compelling, inflamed faith, hope, and charity in order to see Satan's armies take flight and their instruments, which I curse, falling in pieces, what rises from Earth to Heaven-and never does it rise from you so much as when there comes down upon you the horrible scourge of the homicidal, deadly weapons which Satan has taught to man and which man has accepted in setting aside the law which says, 'Love one another as brothers and sisters,'[7] in order to take up the one which says, 'Hate each other as I, Satan, hate'? A chorus of blasphemies, curses, and mockeries of God, of acts of despair. Death often brings to a halt those words on your lips, nails them into you, and carries you off that way, marked by a final sin, in My sight.

Maria, you are amazed that after so much help I should now leave you to feel such anguish. I helped you in the hour of the death of the one you loved[8] and I gave you my heart as a pillow and my mouth as music and linen, which dried your tears with its kiss and relieved your pain with its song of love. But that was your pain. You had already offered it to Me, and I had already used it. It was time for Me to reward you for it. It was time for Me to sustain you because you must serve Me still, my little 'voice,' and I don't want you to die before the moment when your mouth may remain silent, having given enough of my word to undeserving men.

There are now too many who damn themselves in despair and die accusing Me. Even in the mouths of children-

---

7   1 John 3:11-22; 4:11-16
8   Maria's Mother, Iside Fioravanzi on October 4th 1943.

who are today more capable of blaspheming than of praying, of cursing than of smiling, and they will be increasingly capable of blaspheming and cursing, poor flowers sullied by the world and by its infernal king, when theirs is nothing but a still-closed bud.

In order for your utterly excessive curses not to have to be responded to in the end with one by Me which would exterminate you, without giving you time to call upon Me any longer; in order for your utterly excessive accusations against Me not to make Me turn upon you in the end My tremendous accusation; in order for your utterly excessive acts of despair- the natural result of your lives as illegitimate children- not to make Me reply in the end with my eternal condemnation of you, my saved ones who trample upon Me and the salvation I have given you,[9] it is necessary for there to be victims who pray, bless, and hope. But I repeat: let them suffer and suffer from what makes their brothers and sisters suffer; let the victims purify with their loving, suffering, praying, blessing, and hoping the places in which people go to meet Death, not that of the flesh, but of the spirit.

I tell you that if the number of those who love, believe, and hope were equal to the number of those who do not love, do not believe, and do not hope, and if in the tragic moments in which slaughter looms before you an equal number of invocations were to arise alongside the imprecations-note that I am not saying a greater number, but an equal number-all of the snares and wishes of the demons and demon-men would be left shattered and would fall without doing you any more harm, like a vulture whose wings are broken that can no longer plunder.

[9] Hebrews 10:29

Courage! Be someone who saves.

To save! To save Humanity I left Heaven. To save Humanity I experienced death.

To save! The greatest act of charity. The one which was the charity of Christ. The one making you, saviours, the souls that are most Christ-like.

I bless you, O all of you that are sisters to Me in saving. I bless you. I bless you, to whom, in order to make you happy with immeasurable, eternal happiness, I have granted the gift of being someone who saves.

Go in peace. Remain in peace. I am with you, always.»

January 10th 1944: The Spirit Of God.

The Spirit Of God Says:

«Do not fail to call yourself the word of Him who is Wisdom and Love of God, Him who from eternity to eternity pours Himself upon all that is, to sanctify it for God, Him Who with His power presided over all the works of Our Trinity and Who is not foreign to all that is holy in time and in eternity, for I Am the Sanctifier, the One who with His septiform gift sanctifies you and bears you to God, making Him known to you in His will on Earth and in His glory in Heaven.

«I Am the Wisdom of God. I am the One whom the Second Person of our Most Holy Triad calls the 'Teacher of all truth, He who will not speak to you on His own, but will say everything that He has heard and will announce to you the times to come.'[10]

O you that seek to know even more than what is necessary, this is the One Who can give you that knowledge which you seek. I am He. I. Light of Light Am I; Spirit of Spirit Am I; Intelligence of Intelligence. I Am the guardian, the repository of all truths-past, present, and future-the knower of all God's decrees, the

John 16:13

administrator of his lights to men. I am the One who, not absent with my counsel from the Creator's works, not absent from the decree of Redemption, am not absent from you, either, to counsel you and, with the sweetness of love, make the wishes which the Father proposes to you a fait accompli. I am even more. I am the Love inspiring you with what is suitable for giving you God's embrace and bearing you to His breast along the path of holiness.

Like a merciful wet nurse, I clutch your incapacity as those just born to Life and educate and raise you. Holding you in my arms, I give you warmth to bring you to assimilate the most sweet milk of the Word of God so that it will become life in you. I make Myself a shield for you against the dangers of the world and of Satan because Love is a saving power. I guide and support you and, as a master of loving patience, instruct you. I make you- burdensome and sluggish, faint-hearted and weak- into heroes and athletes of God. I make you-spiritually poor-into kings of the spirit, for I cover your spirits with My divine splendors and set them on a throne which is the greatest of all, since Mine is the throne of eternal holiness.

But to know Me it is necessary not to have idolatry in one's heart. It is necessary to believe in what I have sanctified. To believe in the truths which I have illuminated. It is necessary to abandon error. It is necessary to seek God where He is. Not where the Enemy of God and man is.

Do you want to know the Truth? Oh, come to Me! I alone can tell it to you. And I tell it to you in the way my goodness knows to be appropriate for you, so as not to disturb your weakness as men and your relativity.

Why do you love what is contorted, complicated, and dark? Love Me, Who Am simple, straightforward, and luminous, Me, Who Am the joy of God and of the spirit.

Do you want to know the future of the spirit? I teach it to you by speaking to you of an eternity awaiting you in a blessedness which is inconceivable for you, in which, after this hour of sojourn, the only sojourn upon the Earth, you shall rest in God from all labours, from all sorrows, and shall forget pain because Joy shall be your possession; and even if Love, which is never so alive as in Heaven, makes you throb with pain over the living, it shall not be pity which gives you pain, but only active love which shall also be joy.

Do you want to know the Creator's perfections in things, the mysteries of creation? I can tell them to you, I who, as Wisdom, 'emerged first of all from the mouth of God, the firstborn before all creatures[11],' I Who Am in all that is, for everything bears the seal of love, and I Am Love. My Being extends over the whole Universe; My Light bathes the stars, planets, seas, valleys, herbs, and animals in Itself; My Intelligence races over the whole Earth, instructs those far off, gives everyone a reflection of the Exalted, and educates in the search for God; My Charity penetrates like breath and conquers hearts.

I attract the just of the Earth to Myself, and to the upright ones without knowledge of the true God I grant reflections of this holy God of yours whereby a streamlet

---

11   Sirach 24: 5

of Truth is in all revealed religions, placed there by Me, Who Am the One Who irrigates and makes fruitful.

In addition, like the powerful surge of an eternal spring, I overflow on all sides of the Catholic Church of Christ, and with Grace, the seven gifts, and the seven sacraments make faithful Catholics into servants of the Lord, those chosen for the Kingdom, sons and daughters of God, brothers and sisters of Christ, and gods whose destiny is so infinitely sublime that any sacrifice is warranted to possess it.

Turn to Me. You will know and understand and be saved, for you will encounter the Truth. Separate, separate yourselves from error, which gives you no joy or peace. Bend your knee before the true God. Before the God who spoke on Sinai[12] and evangelized in Palestine. Before the God who speaks to you through the Church, made into a Teacher by Me, the Spirit of God.

There is no other God apart from Us: Triune. There is no other Religion but Our centuries-old one. There is no other future, on the Earth and beyond, except the one conveyed to you by the holy Books. Everything else is a Lie destined to be put to shame by Him who is Justice and Truth.

Ask Us-Power, Word, and Wisdom- for light so that you will not walk beyond, along false paths of death, but be able yourselves as well, who are wandering, to come onto the way along which salvation was found by those who, through their humble, wise, holy faith, pleased God, who made them his saints. «

---

12   Exodus 19-20

January 10th 1944: Mary.

Mary Says:

«And since I am the Mother, I also speak, clasping you to my breast to lead you to faith, my children whom I see dying, nourished as you are on deathly poison.

I beg you, for the sake of that Son of mine whom I gave with painful joy for your salvation-come back onto the paths of Christ. You have written His most holy Name on your pathways. But it is a profanation. And if it weren't for the fact that the Enemy obscures your minds and guides your hand, forcing it to write what good sense could not lead you to write, you would not write that blessed Name on the ways over which Satan comes to you and on the doors of your grotesque temples as Godless people.

But for your sake I say to the Father, 'Father, forgive them because they don't know what they are doing[13],' and I ask the Holy Father for you, poor children deceived by Satan. I defeated Satan in myself and for the sake of men. He is under my foot. I will defeat him in you as well, provided you come to me.

---

13   Luke 23, 34

I am the Mother. The Mother whom Love has made the mother of beautiful love. I am the one in whom the manna of Grace rests, as in an ark. I am Full of Grace, nor does God place a limit on my power to pour out this divine treasure. I am the Mother of the Truth, who became flesh in me. I am the bearer of man's Hope. Through me the hope of the patriarchs and the prophets has become a reality. I am the seat of Wisdom, Who made me His own, and the Mother of the Son of God.

Come, that I may take you to Christ, holding your hand, with this hand of mine, which assisted the first steps of Jesus the Saviour along the ways of earth and taught Him to walk so that He would readily go up to Golgotha to save you, dearer to me, because you are the most unfortunate of all men, the condemned, whom I fight to snatch away from the power dragging you into the abyss, to save you for Heaven.

See how much I have wept for you. For you are not the ones who fall when dragged down by a weight of flesh, so impetuous and sudden that it bowls you over without giving you the time or opportunity to react. You are the ones who tenaciously, knowingly commit the sin which is not forgiven-My Son said so[14]. You deny the Truth to make iniquitous lies into truths for yourselves. You become lucifers. And you could be angels!

I don't ask you for much. Only for you to love me as a Mother, only for you to call me. My name will already be honey to your poisoned lips. And it will be salvation, for where Mary is, there Jesus is, and whoever loves me cannot fail to love the Truth who is the Son of My flesh. I do not reproach; I do not condemn. I love. I just love.

---

14   Matthew 12, 32; Mark 3, 29; Luke 12, 10

I should not cause you any fear because I am meeker than an ewe lamb and more peaceful than an olive tree. So meek that, surpassing ewe lambs, I let my Child be torn away from my breast and be sacrificed on an altar of blood without reacting, without cursing. So superior to the olive tree that by myself I made myself an olive under the grindstone, and I let myself be pressed by pain to make the oil to medicate your wounds and consecrate you for Heaven drip out of my virginal, motherly, immaculate heart.

Lay your infirm heads on my lap. I will heal them and say to you the words which Wisdom says to me to lead you to the Light of God.»

January 10th 1944: Maria Valtorta's Witness:

How beautiful! How beautiful! How beautiful what I see is!

I shall try to be very precise and clear in describing for you what Communion brought me. You[15] already know that I was happy. But you don't know what blessedness and what a joyful vision was granted to me from the moment of Eucharistic union on. It was like a picture being shown to me by degrees. But it was not a picture-it was contemplation. I was recollected therein for a good hour with no other prayer but this contemplation, which enraptured me beyond the earth. It began right after receiving the consecrated Host, and I think it did not escape you that I was slow to respond and greet you-I was already enveloped. In spite of that, I expressed the whole act of thanksgiving out loud, as the vision came upon me more and more intensely. And then I became still, with my eyes closed, as if I were sleeping. But I have never been so awake in my entire self as in that hour. In its final stage, the vision is still continuing as I write. I am writing under the gaze of so many heavenly beings who see that I am saying only what I see,

---

15   Her spiritual director, Fr. Romualdo M. Milgliorini

without adding details or making modifications. And here is the vision.

As soon as I received Jesus, I felt the Mother, Mary, on the left-hand side of the bed, who was embracing me with her right arm drawing me to herself. She was wearing her dress and white veil[16], as in the visions of the Grotto, in December. At the same time I felt enveloped by a golden light and by a soft, indescribably soft color, and the eyes of my spirit sought its source, which I sensed was raining down on me from above. It seemed to me that my room, though remaining the room it is, in its floor and four walls and furnishings, no longer had a ceiling and that I was seeing the boundless blue skies of God.

Suspended in these blue skies, the Divine Dove of fire remained perpendicularly over Mary's head, and, of course, over my head, since I was leaning cheek-to-cheek against Mary. The Holy Spirit's wings were open, and He remained in an upright, vertical position. He did not move, and yet He vibrated, and with each vibration there were waves, rays, and sparks of splendor which issued forth. From Him there emerged a cone of golden light whose summit started from the Dove's breast and whose base enwrapped Mary and me. We were gathered into this cone, this cloak, this embrace of joyful light. A most intense light and yet not glaring, for it communicated new strength to one's eyes which increased with every flash flowing forth from the Dove, ever augmenting the flash already existing with every vibration of the Dove. I felt my eyes expanding into a supernatural power, almost as if they were no longer the eyes of a creature, but of an

---

16   Lily white dress ad veil as seen in the Vision of December 29th 1943

already glorified spirit.

When I attained the capacity to see beyond, thanks to the inflamed Love suspended over me, my spirit was called to look higher. And, against the brighter blue of Paradise, I saw the Father. Distinctly, although His figure was in lines of immaterial light. A beauty which I shall not attempt to describe because it is superior to human capacities. He appeared to me as if on a throne. I speak this way because He appeared to me seated with infinite majesty. But I saw no throne, chair, or baldachin*. Nothing resembling the earthly shape of a seat. He appeared to me from my left-hand side (in the direction of my Jesus on the Cross, just to give you an idea, and therefore to the right of His Son), but at an incalculable height.

---

*A canopy made of cloth or stone erected over an altar, shrine or throne in a Christian church.

And yet I saw Him in the most minute of His extremely luminous features. He was looking towards the window (also to give you an idea of the different positions). He was looking with a gaze of infinite love.

I followed His gaze and saw Jesus. Not the Jesus as Teacher I usually see. Jesus as King. White clothing, but with a luminous, extremely white robe, like Mary's. A robe that seems to be made of light. Most beautiful. Stalwart. Imposing. Perfect. Blazing. In His right hand- He was standing-He held His scepter, which is also His standard. A long rod, almost a crosier, but even taller than my very tall Jesus, which doesn't end in the curl of a crosier, but in a transverse rod, which thus forms a cross made in this way, ⊤

from which there hangs, supported by the shorter r⊟ banner of most luminous, white silk, made like this ▽ , and marked on both sides by a purple cross; on the banner, written in words of light, almost as if written with liquid diamonds, is the name «Jesus Christ.»

I very clearly see the wounds on His hands because His right hand is holding the rod aloft, towards the banner, and His left hand is indicating the wound in His side, which I do not, however, see as anything but a luminous point from which there are emanating rays descending to the ground. The wound on the right hand is precisely in the area of the wrist and looks like a glittering ruby the size of a ten-centesimo coin. The one on the left hand is more cer⬭ed and larger, but it further extends like this ⬭ towards the thumb. They shine like vivid rubies. I see no other wounds. On the contrary, the Body of my Lord is most beautiful and intact in all its parts.

The Father is looking at the Son on His left. The Son is looking at his Mother and me. But I assure you that if He were not looking with love, I could not bear the gleaming of His gaze and of His appearance. He is really the King of tremendous majesty who is spoken of[17].

The longer the vision lasts, the more the capacity to perceive the smallest details increases in me and to see further and further all around.

Indeed, after a while I see St. Joseph (in the corner, where the Nativity Scene is). He is not so tall, more or

---

17   in the Roman Liturgy's Dies Irae dies illa (King of Wrath).

less like Mary. Sturdily built. With grizzly hair, curly and short, and a square-cut beard. A long, thin, aquiline nose. Two wrinkles cut across his cheeks, starting from the corners of his nose and moving down until fading at the sides of his mouth in his beard. Dark, very good eyes. In them I rediscover the lovingly good look of my father. The whole face is good, thoughtful without being sad, dignified, but very, very good. He is wearing a dark blue-purple tunic like the petals of certain periwinkles, and his cloak is the color of camel's skin. Jesus points him out to me, saying, «Here is the patron of all the just.»

The Light then calls my spirit from the other side of the room-that is, towards Marta's bed[18]-and I see my angel. He is kneeling, facing towards Mary, whom he seems to venerate. Dressed in white. His arms are crossed over his chest, and his hands are touching his shoulders. His head is bending very low, and I thus see little of his face. His gesture reflects profound devotion. I see his beautiful, long, extremely white, pointed wings, real wings made to fly swiftly and surely from Earth to Heaven, now gathered in behind his back. By his attitude he is teaching me how to say, «Hail Mary.»

As I continue to observe him, I sense that someone is close to me on my right and is resting his hand on my right shoulder. It is my St. John, with his face shining with cheerful love.

I feel blessed. And I recollect myself in the midst of such blessedness, thinking I have touched the peak. But a brighter gleaming of the Spirit of God and of the wounds of Jesus, my Lord, further increases my ability to see.

---

18   Marta lived with and lovingly cared for Maria from 1935 until her death in1961.

And I see the heavenly Church, the triumphant Church! I shall attempt to describe it for you.

Above there remain the Father, the Son, and now the Spirit as well, high above the Two, half way between the Two, whom He links with his splendors.

Further down, as if between two sky-blue slopes- a blue which is not of this earth-gathered together in a blessed valley, is the multitude of those glorified in Christ, the army of those marked with the name of the Lamb,(Revelation 7) a multitude which is light, a light which is song, a song which is adoration, an adoration which is blessedness.

On the left are the ranks of the confessors. On the right are those of the virgins. I did not see the ranks of the martyrs, and the Spirit has me understand that the martyrs are added to the virgins, for martyrdom renders the soul virginal once more, as if just created. All of them seem to be dressed in white, both the confessors and the virgins. That luminous white of the robes of Jesus and Mary.

Light emanates from the sky-blue floor and the sky-blue walls of the holy valley, almost as if they were made of burning sapphire. The robes of diamond cloth emit light, as do, above all, the spiritualized bodies and faces. And here I shall make an effort to describe for you what I have observed in the different bodies. Only the bodies of Jesus and Mary are bodies of flesh and spirit- alive, pulsating, perfect, sensitive to touch and contact: two glorious bodies which are, however, really «bodies.» The Eternal Father, the Holy Spirit, and my angel are light in the shape of a body, just so it can be perceptible to this poor servant of God. St. Joseph and St. John are light which is now more compact, certainly because I must perceive their presence and words. All the blessed forming the host of the Heavens are white flames which are spiritualized bodies.

None of the confessors turns around. They are all looking at the Most Holy Trinity. Some of the virgins turn about. I distinguish the Apostles Peter and Paul, for, though luminous and dressed in white like everyone else, their faces are indeed more distinguishable than the others- a characteristic Jewish face. They are looking at me benignly (it's a good thing they are!).

Then there are three blessed spirits, who I grasp are women, who observe me, gesture, and smile. You could say they are inviting me. They are young. But it in fact seems to me that all the blessed are of the same age: youthful, perfect, and equally beautiful. They are lesser copies of Jesus and Mary. I cannot say who these three heavenly creatures are, but since two are carrying palms and one, only flowers- the palms are the only sign distinguishing the martyrs from the virgins- I think I am not mistaken in saying they are Agnes, Cecilia, and Therese of Lisieux.

In spite of my desire to do so, what I cannot convey to you is the Hallelujah of this multitude. A Hallelujah which is both powerful and soft as a caress. And everything laughs and shines more intensely with each hosanna of the multitude for its God.

The vision ceases and in its intensity crystallizes in this form. Mary leaves me, and, with Her, John and Joseph; Mary takes her place in front of the Son, and the other two, theirs, in the ranks of the virgins.

Praise be to Jesus Christ.

January 11ᵗʰ 1944: John.

12:15 A.M:

John Says:

«Instructed as I was, penetrated by and made one with the Master, in my Gospel there lives the Word just as it was spoken, for, on account of my union, I was able to repeat it without modifications. It is Christ who speaks. John is nothing but the instrument who writes. Just like you[19].

Ours is a great destiny, to which one must be faithful even in the smallest details so as not to contaminate divine doctrine with ourselves as creatures, and for the sake of this destiny we must lead a chaste life so that the Word may descend where there is nothing impure, not even the shadow of a thought.

To receive the Word of God is like receiving the Bread of Heaven. He is the Bread of Heaven who becomes a Word for us so as to become Bread in the spirits of our brothers and sisters. He is the Eucharist of the Word, no less holy than the Eucharist of the altar, for, on coming into us, the Eucharistic Christ brings us His Word, which is heard more or less clearly to the extent that the life of the spirit is in us, and, on coming into us, Christ the Master brings us His nourishment, which renders us

---

[19]   In fact, Maria Valtorta was called «Little John

increasingly capable of making the Eucharist the Food of eternal life.

«He, my Master and yours, said so: 'Blessed are those who keep the Word of God in their hearts.' And He also said, 'Whoever listens to my Word has eternal life,' and 'I am the living Bread descending from Heaven. Whoever feeds on Me will not die, and I will raise him up on the last day[20].' The Master, then, gives a single destiny to whoever feeds on Him- the Word of the Father and the Bread of Heaven.

But I am not speaking so much to you for your sake, disciple who are in the light. I-a light of Christ, of Christ, the Light of the world- am speaking to the ones in darkness, who, like those with scales over their pupils, go groping in the dark and are unable to get onto the path where the Master is passing by; they don't want to get onto it and cry out, 'Jesus, save us! Give us your Light!'

If they called Him, He would come to them; He would stay in them and give them the blessed destiny of becoming children of God, born a second time- the only time people can be reborn-, not in the flesh, which, when lifeless, will never again clothe the spirit that has had it as a robe, except on the last day, when the spirit will go with it to glory or damnation, but in the spirit, which is regenerated by becoming inserted into Christ, for Christ, on possessing it in Himself, as part of His most holy Being, joins it to the Spirit of God, Who is the One who enables us to be reborn, no longer as men, but as children of God-and they would know the Light and separate themselves from Darkness and Deceit, for Christ is Truth and Christ is Light, and the Paraclete,

---

20   Luke11.28; John 6 :22-29

Whom Christ gives to those who are 'His,' is Light and Truth, and whoever has Christ has the Truth and the Light of the Triune Divinity in himself.

Leave the eternal Killer, who perished and leads others to perish, for he did not persevere in the truth which, in his fortunate angelic destiny, he had possessed from the first instant of his creation. Believe in Christ, who cannot lie, for He is God and has God's Perfection.

He tells you over and over again: 'I will raise you up.' Could He say an improper word-He, Perfect in Knowledge and Intelligence? He says, 'I will raise you up'; He does not say, 'I will reincarnate you.' And He specifies 'on the last day' and further states, 'As the Father raises the dead and restores them to life, so, too, the Son gives life to whoever He wills... Whoever listens to my word and believes in the One who sent me has eternal life and does not undergo condemnation, but passes from death to life... The time is coming when the dead will hear the voice of the Son of God, and whoever has heard it will live. The time is coming when all those in the tombs will hear the voice of the Son of God and come out-those who did good, to the resurrection of life; those who did evil, to the resurrection of death[21].'

Therefore, He who is Truth and Knowledge states, repeats, insists, and swears regarding one life, one alone, of the flesh, and one life, one alone, of the spirit. This life is led in our one day as man and then, only on the last day, at the command of the God Jesus, the flesh rises again to clothe the spirit whose robe it was. This eternal life is obtained only by means of our one day, and if during it we have slain the spirit once, never again can it

---

21   John 17-47

become reincarnated to pass from death to life through successive stages.

No. The power of God the Father, of God the Son, Jesus, and of God the Spirit Paraclete, can give you the resurrection of the spirit on earth through a miracle of grace, or through the intercession of a 'saint,' on earth or in Heaven, or through your desire to rise again as well. But this happens here, on Earth, in your one day. Once dusk has come for you and you have entered into the sleep of the human night, there is no longer a possible resurrection through new stages of life. If you are among the spiritually dead, there is only death.

I, a disciple of Christ, I, who have seen the future life beyond life and the final resurrection, swear to you that this is true.

Get free from these chains. They are the most dangerous ones which Satan hurls at you. Take the first step to say to Christ, 'I am coming to You,' and to Satan, 'Back, in the name of Jesus.' Receive the first truth.

You cannot know how sweet the Lord is- the good Master, the holy Shepherd- to those turning to Him. Like a father, He clasps you to His heart and instructs you, cares for you, and feeds you. Do not say that you love Him. You do not love Him in truth and therefore do not love Him.

The truth is in His Gospel. The Gospel is the one spoken by Him to his disciples and the one He continues to confirm and explain, through His benignity as the Saviour. Always the same after so many centuries. There is no other.

If there were a second life, or several others, He would have said so. You are not Parsees* or Shintoists**-you are

'Christians.' Abandon, then, the chimeras, errors, and deceits which Satan prompts to wrest you away from God and believe in what Christ has said.

*Member of the Zoroastrian group.
** Japanese religion.

Whoever loves believes. Whoever loves little doubts. Whoever does not love accepts a contrary doctrine. The doctrine you follow is contrary to that of Jesus Christ, the Word of God, our Master, the Light of the world. You do not, then, love Christ in truth.»

January 11th 1944: The Apostle Paul.

10 A.M

The Apostle Paul[22] Says:

«The ancient pagans for whom I broke the bread of the Faith seem to be alive still- indeed, to have returned, according to your belief, to be reincarnated with their ancient theories regarding the resurrection and the second life- to such an extent the theory of reincarnation is still incarnate- and now more than ever- and ingrown in your minds, after twenty centuries of preaching the Gospel.

The only thing that is reincarnated is this theory of yours, which flourishes again like mold in alternating periods of spiritual obscurity. For- realize this, O you that think you are the most spiritually evolved- this is the sign of a spiritual decline and not of a dawn of the spirit. The lower the Sun of God is in your spirits, the more there are formed larvae in the rising shadow, and fevers stagnate, and the bearers of death swarm, and the spores that eat into, corrode, absorb, and destroy the life of your spirits

---

22   In Acts 17: 22-31: Greeks believed in metempsychosis or transmigration of souls.
In 1 Corinthians, chapter 15, Paul argues for the resurrection that differentiates reincarnation by this statement: «As men die only once after that to face judgment, so Christ, having offered once to take away the sins of many, will appear a second time to those who are waiting to give them salvation «(Hebrews 9, 27)

germinate, as in hyperborean woods where the night lasts for six months and turns the thickets- filled with vegetable and animal life- into dead areas like those of a world without life.

Fools! The dead do not come back. With any new body. There is just one resurrection: the last one.

You are not- you that are made in the image and likeness of God- no, you are not seeds that in alternating cycles sprout and become stems, flowers, fruits, and seeds, and, starting from the seeds, stems, flowers, and fruit. You are men, not grass in the field. You are destined for Heaven, not to a horse's stall. You possess the spirit of God, that spirit which God infuses into you through his continuous spiritual generation, which responds to human generation of new flesh.

And what do you think? That God, our Almighty, unlimited, eternal God, has a limit in His generating? A limit which dictates that He create a given number of spirits and no more, so that, to continue the life of men on earth, like a sales clerk in a department store, He has to go to the shelves and search among the spirits heaped up there for one to be reused for that specific merchandise; or, even better, do you think He is like a scribe who exhumes a certain document and looks for a given scroll because the time has come to record an event?

O fools, fools, fools! You are not merchandise, parchment, or seeds. You are men.

The body, like a seed, falls, when its cycle is over, into the corruption of the tomb. The spirit returns to its Source to be judged as to whether it is alive or as putrid as the flesh, and, in accordance with its state of being, it goes to its destiny. Nor does it emerge from that destiny any more except to call what was its own to a single resurrection, in which those who were putrid in life become perfectly putrid forever, with that corrupt spirit and that corrupt flesh which they had in their one, unrepeatable life; and those who were 'just' in life rise again, glorious and incorruptible, elevating their flesh to the glory of their glorious spirits, spiritualizing it, divinizing it, for through it and with it they have overcome, and it is right that they should triumph with it.

Here you are rational animals because of the spirit you possess, which obtains life for the flesh it overcomes as well. In the other life you will be spirits vivifying the flesh which has obtained victory by remaining subject to the spirit. The animal nature always comes first. This is the true evolution. But it is single. Then, from animal nature, which has been able to lighten itself through threefold virtue, there comes spiritual nature.

In accordance with the way you live in this life, such you will be in the second one. If what is heavenly has prevailed in you, you will know the nature of God in yourselves and possess this nature because God will be your eternal possession. If you have had a predominance of the earthly, beyond death you will know dullness, death, cold, horror, and darkness- all that is common to the body which is lowered into the grave, with this difference: the duration of this second, true death is eternal.

As the heirs of God by God's will, O brothers and sisters, do not allow yourselves to lose this inheritance by following flesh and blood and mental error.

I, too, erred and was contrary to Truth; I was a persecutor of Christ. My sin is always before me, even in the glory of this kingdom, whose gates were opened to me by my repentance, my faith, and my martyrdom because I confessed Christ and immortal life. But when the Light cast me down, making itself known, I abandoned error to follow the Light[23].

The Light has made itself known to you by way of twenty centuries of prodigies, undeniable even for the fiercest deniers and the most obstinate. Why, then, do you fortunate ones who have twenty centuries of divine manifestations as witness to that Light wish to remain in error?

I, a witness to Christ, swear this to you. Neither flesh nor blood can inherit the kingdom of God, but only the spirit can. And, as is stated in the Gospel of Jesus our Lord[24], the children of this age- understand, O brothers and sisters, that here 'age' signifies those who are in the world, that is, those who are earthly- are not the ones destined to rise again and remarry, possessing a second earthly life. Only those who are worthy of the second age, the eternal one, will rise again- that is, those who will no longer be able to die, having already lived, but who, in having obtained spiritual life and having become like the angels and sons and daughters of the Most High, no longer hunger for human marriage, but with their spirits desire one union alone: union with God as Love; one possession alone: the possession of God; one dwelling alone: the heavenly one; and one life alone: life in Life.

---

23   Acts 9:1-22
24   Matthew 22:23-33; Mark 12: 18-27; Luke 20:27-40

Christian Tenets

Amen, amen, amen!»

January 17ᵗʰ 1944: Jesus.

Jesus Says:

«Take into consideration - more than for yourself and for many like you - that this dictation falls within the group of the 'seven dictations'[25]. When one has begun to undermine a system, it is good to continue with the blows of a battering ram. And this form of thought is a system hard as steel.. One must persist to overcome.

There is only one Faith which is true. Mine. Just as I have given it to all of you- a divine gem whose light is life. It is not enough to remain in that faith nominally, just as a piece of marble placed in a room by chance remains. But it is necessary to fuse oneself with it and make it Part of yourselves.

Is the clothing you wear life for you? Does it perhaps become your flesh and blood? No. It is attire which is useful for you, but if you take it off to don other apparel, you remove nothing from your interior. Whereas the food you eat becomes your blood and your flesh, and you can no longer remove it from yourselves. It is a part - and an essential one - of yourselves, for without blood and flesh

---

25   On Reincarnation or metempsychosis, as in the final passage for January 11ᵗʰ.

you could not live, and without food you would not have flesh and blood.

The same occurs with Faith. It must not be something resting upon you at certain hours, like a veil for the purpose of appearing more attractive and seducing one's brothers, but it must be an intrinsic part of you, inseparable from you, vital in you. Faith is not just hope for things believed in; faith is a life reality. A life beginning here, in this chimera of human life, and fulfilled in the hereafter, in that eternal life which awaits you.

Today a great heresy is taking place, a supremely sacrilegious heresy[26]. The son of Satan[27], one of the sons, whom I could call one of the greatest, not the greatest one in the past, who is Judas, not the greatest one to come, who will be the Antichrist, but one of those living now for the punishment of man, who has worshipped man and not God[28], dealing out death to himself by way of man, whereas I, God, gave man Life by way of my death - meditate on this difference .

The son of Satan proclaims a new faith which is a tragic, sacrilegious, accursed parody of my Faith[29]. A new gospel

[26] Nazism attempting at this time to establish a religion to replace Christianity as we will discover gradually.

[27] Hitler

[28] For Nazism and fascism, but also to Marxism-Leninism and many movements of the time that will lead to the destruction of many countries and the death of millions of people.

[29] In 1920 the National Socialist party advocates «positive Christianity» that will become the mainstream of the Third Reich at the instigation of Alfred Rosenberg and Heinrich Himmler. The goal of positive Christianity was to cut the Jewish roots of Christianity and religion create a transition between Christianity and paganism who successfully complete the Aryan cult. This positive Christianity was related to any dominant faiths Germany: Catholicism and Protestant-

is proclaimed; a new church is founded; a new altar is raised up; a new cross[30] is set on high; a new sacrifice is celebrated. Man's gospel, church, altar, cross, and sacrifice. Not God's.

There is one Gospel: Mine.

There is one Church: Mine, Roman Catholic.

There is one Altar: the one consecrated by oil, water, and wine, the one founded upon the bones of a martyr and saint of God[31].

There is one Cross: Mine. The one from which the Body of the Son of God - Jesus Christ - is hanging, the one reproducing the figure of the wood I bore with infinite love and such great fatigue up to the summit of Calvary. There are no other crosses. There may be other signs, hieroglyphics like the ones sculpted upon the Pharaohs' hypogea or upon the Aztecs' stems - signs, nothing more than signs, of man or Satan, but not crosses, not a symbol of a whole poem of love, redemption, and victory over all the forces of Evil, of whatever kind.

---

ism.
This ideology is also condemned, March 10, 1937 in the encyclical Mit Sorge brennender.
Positive Christianity is gradually moving towards a specifically Germanic cult with its celebrations (Lebenfeiern), calendar replacing the Christian calendar and its public festivals.
In December 1941, Pius XII denounced in a message broadcast manufacture all parts «of Christianity in their image, a new idol in which there is no salvation [...] a new religion without soul, or soul without religion, a form of Christianity death, deprived of the spirit of Christ. «

30   Referring to the Nazi swastika

31   At the dedication of a church, otherwise known dedication, relics of martyrs and other saints are sealed in the altar as a sign of the unity of the Mystical Body in Christ. This people, the interior walls and the altar are sprinkled with holy water. The altar is consecrated by anointing with chrism (holy oil). The Eucharist is celebrated then.

Christian Tenets

From the time of Moses until now, and from now until the moment of Judgment[32], there will be one cross: the one like mine, the one which first bore 'the serpent,[33]' a symbol of eternal life, the one which bore Me, the one I shall bear with Me when I appear to you as the Judge and King to judge everyone: you, O my blessed ones who believe in my Sign and my Name; and you, accursed ones, parodists and sacrilegious, who have forcefully removed my Sign and my Name from churches, states, and consciences, replacing them with your Satanic symbol and your name as Satanic ones.

There is one Sacrifice: the one mystically repeating my own, and in the bread and wine it gives you my Body and my Blood immolated for you. There is no other body or blood which can replace the Great Victim. And the blood and the bodies that you immolate, O ferocious sacrificers of those who are subject to you and at your disposal- for you have turned them into the bodies of galley slaves condemned to row, marked with your sign as if they were beasts to be slaughtered, rendered unable even to think, for you have robbed, suppressed, and stricken this sovereignty of man over the brutes, and you crack the whip over them and threaten them with 'death' if they so much as dare, even inwardly alone, to judge you - and this blood and these bodies do not celebrate, do not substitute, and are not of use, no, for sacrifice.

Mine obtains graces and blessings for you. This one obtains condemnation and eternal curses for you. I hear and see the moans and the tortures of the oppressed whom you slaughter in soul and mind even more than in body. Not one of your subjects is safe from your knife,

32   Matthew 25:31-46
33   Numbers 21:4-9, John 3:14-15

which empties them of freedom, peace, serenity, and faith and makes them moral dimwits, frightened, desperate, and rebellious. I hear and see the death rattle of the slain and the blood bathing 'your' altar. Poor blood, for which I have a mercy surpassing all measure and whose error, too, I forgive, for man has already punished himself thereby, and God does not rage where there has already been expiation.

But I swear to you that I will make that blood and those moans your eternal torment. You shall eat, regurgitate, and vomit blood; you shall choke in it; your souls shall be deafened by those death rattles and those moans to the point of madness, and you shall be obsessed by millions of ghostly faces that will shout at you the millions of crimes you have committed and curse you. You shall find this in the place where your father, the king of deceit and cruelty, is awaiting you.

And where among you is the Pontiff, the Priest for the celebration of the rite? You are executioners and not priests. That is not an altar - it is a scaffold. That is not a sacrifice - it is a blasphemy. That is not a faith - it is a sacrilege.

Come down, O accursed ones, before I fulminate you with a horrendous death. At least die the death of beasts, that withdraw into their burrows to die, sated with prey. Do not wait on that pedestal of yours as hellish gods for Me to hand you over to expiation- not of the spirit, but of your beastly bodies - and have you die in the midst of the mockery of the throng and the cruelty of those who are now being tortured. There is a limit. I remind you. And there is no mercy for those aping God and becoming like

Lucifer[34].

And you, O peoples, manage to be strong in Truth and Justice.

Human philosophies and human doctrines are all contaminated with dross. The current ones are filled with venom. One should not play with poisonous snakes. The time comes when the snake emerges from the charm and administers a fatal bite. Do not let yourselves be poisoned.

Remain united to Me. In Me there is justice, peace, and love. Do not seek other doctrines. Live out the Gospel. You will be happy. Live by Me, in Me. You will not experience the great bodily joys. I do not confer them- I confer the true joys which are not just the enjoyment of the flesh, but also of the spirit, the honest, blessed, holy joys which I have granted and sanctioned, the ones in which I did not refuse to take part.

The family, children, an honest well-being, a prosperous and peaceful homeland, real harmony with one's brothers and sisters and with the nations. This is what I call holy and what I bless. Therein you also possess health, for family life, when honestly lived out, gives health to the body; therein you possess serenity, for a business or a profession, when honestly engaged in, provide tranquility of conscience; therein you have the peace and prosperity of your homeland and town, for, when living in real harmony with your countrymen and with neighbouring peoples, you avoid resentments and wars.

In your blood Satan's venom ferments, I know, my poor children. But I have given you Myself as an antidote. I

---

34   Isaiah 14:9-15

have taught you to engrave my Sign, which overcomes Satan, upon yourselves, in yourselves.

Circumcise your spirits with Me. A much higher and more perfect circumcision! It removes from your flesh those cells in which the germs of death settle and implants in you the Life that I am. It strips you of animality and robes you in Christ. It buries you as children of blameworthy Adam- and you are also blameworthy yourselves because of original sin and your own sins- in Baptism and the Confession of Christ and makes you rise again as children of the Most High.

Do not separate from Me. Oh, I shall certainly take you into the Heavens if you remain part of Me, and, in addition- since not all of you are 'heaven,' but a little of the Earth's mire always remains in you -look, I promise you that the Father's blessing will not be lacking even upon your mire, for the Father can only bless his Son, and my Power shall overshadow you to such a degree- if you remain in Me, if you pray with Me. saying 'our Father' just as I taught you[35]86- that the Father will give you both the Kingdom of Heaven, as is requested in the first part, and your daily bread and the forgiveness of sins, as is requested in the second.

If you remain in Me, like children in their mother's womb, our Father will be able to see only the robe which robes you: Me, your Redeemer, the one generating you for Heaven and His Son; and upon His Son, the object of all His pleasure, for whom He has made, in addition to all things, forgiveness and glory, too, for the joy of His Son, who wants you to be forgiven and glorious, He will make His graces rain down.

---

35 Matthew 6:9-13, Luke 11:2-4

Christian Tenets

I destroyed your death with mine. I annulled your sins with my Blood. I redeemed them beforehand for your sake. I have made everything powerless to harm you in the future life by nailing your sin- from Adam on to every one of you- to my cross. I can say I consumed all the world's poison by tasting of the sponge soaked in gall and vinegar on Golgotha and turned that Evil into Good for you, since, in dying thereby, I distilled it, and made the deathly mixture water of Life flowing from my torn chest.

Remain in Me with purity and fortitude. Do not be hypocrites, but sincere in Faith. It is not external practices that constitute faith and love. Even the sacrilegious have these and make use of them to deceive you and obtain human glories for themselves. You must not be like this.

Remember that, as I have regenerated you to the Life of Grace, to which you were dead, so I have raised you up with Me to eternal Life. Look, then, at that place of Life. Seek all the things which are currency for you to enter therein. All the things of the spirit: Faith, Hope, Charity, and the other virtues which make man a child of God.

Seek the unerring Science: the one contained in my doctrine. This is the one which makes you capable of orienting yourselves in such a way that Heaven will be yours.

Seek Glory. Not the ludicrous and often blameworthy glory of the earth, which I frequently condemn and never deem to be true glory, but only a mission which God gives you so that you will turn it into a means to reach heavenly Glory. True Glory is obtained by overturning the world's values. The world says, 'Enjoy, stockpile, be proud, overbearing, heartless, hate in order to overcome, lie in order to be successful, commit cruelties in order to domineer.' I say to you, 'Be moderate, continent, without thirst for flesh, gold, or power; be sincere, honest, humble, loving, patient, meek, and merciful[36].87 Forgive those who offend you, love those who hate you, help those who are less fortunate than you. Love, love, love.'

In truth, I tell you that not a single act of love, though minimal, such as a sigh of compassion for someone suffering, shall go unrewarded. A boundless reward in Heaven. And now a great reward, not comprehensible except for the one experiencing it, even on earth. The reward of the peace of Christ for all my good ones, of the luminousness of the Word for the 'very good ones' into whom I come to find my comfort.

My dear children, whom I love with a love much greater than all the hatred circulating like a hellish liquid over the Earth, love Me, in turn; whatever you do or say, do it in the name of your Jesus, thus giving thanks, by means of Him, to God your Father, and the grace of the Lord will remain over you like a shield on earth and a secure halo for Heaven.»

Maria Valtorta's Note:

That «address» was delivered about eight days ago- around the 10th or 11th of this month, then. The following declaration was made therein, after other, varied statements: that priests are not necessary for either God or souls because they are moneygrubbers and so on and so forth and that, when the war is over- with

---

36   Matthew 5: 3-12, Luke 6:20-23

Christian Tenets

the victory of Germany, of course- a new, true worship will be established and new, true temples will be opened, and there the faithful of the new religion will go to witness the consummation of the sacrifice in which the bread given to the Germanic people and its blood will be brought.

Hitler's words and promises for his subjects.

May 25th 1944: Maria Valtorta's Witness.

I shall attempt to describe the inexpressible, ineffable, beatific vision in the late evening yesterday, the one that led me from the dream of the soul to that of the body in order to appear to me even clearer and more beautiful when I returned to my senses. And before undertaking this description, which will remain farther from reality than we are from the sun, I wondered, «Should I write first or do my penance?» I was longing to write what brings me joy, and I know that after the penance I am slower in the material labour of writing. But the voice of light of the Holy Spirit- this is what I call it, for it is immaterial, like the light, and yet as bright as the most blazing light and for my spirit writes its words, which are sound and flaring and joy, joy, joy- tells me, enwrapping my soul in its flashing of love, «First penance and then the writing of what constitutes your joy. Penance must always precede everything, in you, for it is what merits joy for you. Every vision arises from a prior penance, and every penance opens the way for every higher contemplation. You live for this reason. You are loved for this reason. You will be blessed for this reason. Sacrifice, sacrifice. Your way, your mission, your strength, your glory. «

I then did all my daily penances first. But I did not even feel them. The eyes of my spirit were «seeing» the sublime vision, and it was annulling bodily sensitivity. I thus understand the reason why the martyrs could smilingly endure those horrid tortures. If for me, so inferior to them in virtue, a contemplation, spreading from my spirit to my bodily senses, can annul sensitivity to pain in them, for them, as perfect in love as a human creature can be, and seeing the Perfection of God unveiled, because of their perfection, a real annihilation of material weaknesses must have occurred. The joy of the vision annulled the indigence of the flesh, sensitive to all suffering.

And now I shall try to describe:

I have seen Paradise again[37]. And I have understood what its Beauty, Nature, Light, and Song are made of. Everything, in short. Its Works, too, which, from such a height, inform, regulate, and provide for the whole created universe. As on the previous occasion, in the early days of this year, I believe, I have seen the Most Holy Trinity. But let us proceed in orderly fashion.

Even the eyes of the spirit- though much more capable of withstanding the Light than the poor eyes of the body, which cannot look fixedly at the sun, a star like the little flame of a smoking wick as compared to the Light which is God- need to accustom themselves by degrees to contemplation of this lofty Beauty.

God is so good that, though wanting to reveal Himself in His splendors, He does not forget that we are poor spirits still imprisoned in flesh and thus weakened by this imprisonment. Oh, how lovely, shining, and sparkling

---

37   Seen on January 10th

are the spirits God creates at every instant to be souls for new creatures! I have seen them, and I know. But we... until we return to Him, cannot withstand all the Splendor at once. And He, in His goodness, draws us towards it by degrees.

First of all, then, last night I saw a sort of immense rose. I say «rose» to provide an idea of these circles of jubilant light that centered increasingly around a point of unbearable splendour.

A boundless rose! Its light was that which it received from the Holy Spirit. The most radiant light of eternal Love. Topaz and liquid gold turned into a flame... Oh, I don't know how to explain! He shone forth on high, on high and alone, set in the immaculate and most radiant sapphire of the Empyrean, and from Him the Light descended in unending waves. The Light which penetrated the rose of the blessed and the angelic choirs and rendered it luminous with its light, which is nothing but the product of the light of the Love penetrating it. But I did not distinguish saints or angels. I saw only the immeasurable festoons of the circles of the celestial flower.

I was already entirely blissful and would have blessed God for His goodness when, instead of crystallizing that way, the vision opened into broader splendours, as if coming closer and closer to me, enabling me to observe it with my spiritual eyes, now accustomed to the first splendour and capable of withstanding a brighter one.

And I saw God the Father: Radiance in the radiance of Paradise. Lines of most radiant light, extremely white, incandescent. Just think: if I was able to distinguish Him in that sea of light, what must His Light have been like, which, though surrounded by so much additional light, annulled it, turning it into a kind of reflected shadow compared to its splendor? Spirit... Oh, how one sees that it is spirit! It is All. So perfect that it is All. It is nothing because not even the touch of any other spirit in Paradise could touch God. A most perfect Spirit, even in His immateriality. Light, Light, nothing but Light.

In front of God the Father was God the Son. In the robe of His glorified Body, upon which there shone the royal garb covering His most holy Members without concealing His super-indescribable beauty. Majesty and Goodness fused into this Beauty of His. The carbuncles of His five Wounds shot forth five swords of light over all of Paradise and increased its splendour and that of His glorified Person.

He had no halo or crown of any kind. But His whole Body emitted light, that special light of spiritualized bodies, which in Him and in the Mother is extremely intense and issues forth from His Flesh, which is flesh, but not opaque, like ours. Flesh which is light. This light condenses even more around his Head. Not into a halo, I repeat, but from His whole Head. His smile was light, and His gaze, light, light piercing from His most beautiful Brow, without wounds. But it seemed that, in the places where the thorns had once drawn blood and brought pain, there transuded brighter luminosity now.

Jesus was standing, holding His royal banner, as in the vision I had in January, I believe.

A little below Him, very little, comparable to a step on an ordinary stairway, was the Most Blessed Virgin. As lovely as She is in Heaven- that is, with her perfect human beauty glorified into heavenly beauty.

She was standing between the Father and the Son, who were a few meters apart (Just to use sensory comparisons). She was in the middle and with her hands crossed over her breast- her gentle, snow-white, small, very lovely hands- and her face slightly upraised- her tender, perfect, loving, very delicate face- was gazing at the Father and the Son in adoration.

Filled with veneration, She was looking at the Father. She did not say a word. But her whole gaze was a voice of adoration and prayer and song. She was not kneeling. But She was so worshipful that her gaze made Her more prostrate than in the deepest genuflection. She was saying, «Sanctus!» and «I adore You!» with her look alone.

Filled with love, She was gazing at her Jesus. She did not say a word. But her whole gaze was a caress; every caress of her soft eyes was saying, «I love You!» She was not seated. She did not touch her Son. But her gaze received Him as if He were on her lap, surrounded by her motherly arms, just as- and more than- in His Childhood and Death. She was saying, «My Son!» and «My joy!» and «My love!» with her look alone.

She took delight in gazing at the Father and the Son. And from time to time She would uplift her face and gaze even more to seek out the Love that was shining high above Her, perpendicularly. And then its dazzling light, made of a pearl turned into light, became ignited as if a flame were assailing it to set it on fire and make it more beautiful. She would receive the kiss of Love and reach out with all her humility and purity, with her charity, to respond with a caress to the Caress and say, «Here I am. I am your Bride and I love You and am yours. Yours for eternity,» And the Spirit would flame forth more brightly when Mary's gaze would merge with His splendors.

And Mary would turn her glance back to the Father and the Son. It seemed that, having been made the repository of Love, She was distributing it. What a poor image I convey! I shall state it better. It seemed that the Spirit was choosing Her to be the one who, gathering all Love into Herself, would then bear it to the Father and the Son so that the Three would join and kiss one another, becoming One. Oh, the joy of comprehending this poem of love! And to see the mission of Mary, the Seat of Love!

But the Spirit did not concentrate His splendours on Mary alone. Our Mother is great. Second only to God. But can a basin, even if very large, contain the ocean? No. It is filled and overflows. But the ocean has water for the whole earth. Such is the Light of Love. And It was descending in a perpetual caress upon the Father and the Son, clasping Them in a ring of splendour. And it expanded further, after having been beatified by contact with the Father and the Son, who responded with love to Love, and extended over all of Paradise.

And Paradise was thus revealed in its details... There were angels. Higher than the blessed, circles around the Hub of Heaven that is the Triune God, with the virginal Gem of Mary as its heart. They more vividly resemble God the Father. Perfect and eternal spirits, they are outlines of light, inferior only to that of God the Father, with an indescribable form of beauty. They adore... They send forth harmonies. With what? I do not know. Perhaps with the heartbeat of their love. For there are not words; and the lines of their mouths do not shift their luminosity. They shine like motionless waters struck by bright sun. But their love is a song. And it is such a sublime harmony that only a grace of God can allow one to hear it without dying of joy.

Below are the blessed. These, in their spiritualized appearance, bear a closer resemblance to the Son and Mary. They are more compact, perceptible to the eye, I would say, and- I get the impression- to touch than the angels are. But they are still immaterial. Physical traits are, however, more marked in them and distinguish them from each other. I therefore understand whether someone is an adult or a child, a man or a woman. I do not see old people, in the sense of decrepitude. It seems that even when the spiritualized bodies belong to those who have died at an advanced age, the signs of the decay of our flesh cease up above. There is more grandeur in an elderly man than in a young, person. But not that dreariness of wrinkles, baldness, toothless mouths, and curved backs proper to human beings. The maximum age seems to be forty or forty-five- that is, flourishing virility, even if the gaze and appearance possess patriarchal dignity.

Among the many- how large a people of saints... and how large a people of angels! The circles fade away, becoming a wake of light through the deep blue splendours of a boundless immensity! And from afar, from afar, from this celestial horizon there still comes the sound of the sublime alleluia, and the light flickers which is the love of this army of angels and the blessed...

Among the many I see an imposing spirit this time. Tall, severe, but good. With a long beard that flows half-way down his chest and with tablets in his hands. The tablets look like the waxen ones the men of old used to write on. He is supporting himself on them with his left hand and holding them, in turn, against his left knee. I don't know who he is. I think of Moses or Isaiah. I don't know why That's what I think. He looks at me and smiles with great dignity. Nothing else. But what eyes! Made precisely to dominate the throngs and penetrate the secrets of God.

My spirit is becoming increasingly capable of seeing in the Light. And I see that with every fusion of the three Persons, a fusion which is repeated with a pressing, incessant rhythm, as if spurred by an insatiable hunger for love, the unceasing miracles which are God's works are produced.

I see that the Father, out of love for the Son, to whom He wants to give an ever greater number of followers, creates souls. Oh, how beautiful! They emerge like sparks, like petals of light, like globe-shaped gems in a way I am unable to describe, from the Father. It is an incessant issuing forth of new souls... Beautiful, joyous in descending to pervade a body out of obedience to their Author. How lovely they are when they emerge from God! I do not see - I cannot see while I am in Paradise - when original sin sullies them.

The Son, out of zeal for his Father, without pause receives and judges those who, when life is over, return to the Origin to be judged. I do not see these spirits. I understand whether they are judged with joy, mercy, or implacability from the changes in Jesus' expression. What a radiant smile when a saint presents himself to Him! What a light of sad mercy when He must separate Himself from someone who has to be cleansed before entering the Kingdom! What a flash of offended, painful indignation when He must repudiate a rebel forever!

It is here that I understand what Paradise is. And what

its Beauty, Nature, Light, and Song are made of. It is made by Love. Paradise is Love. It is Love that creates everything therein. Love is the foundation on which everything rests. Love is the apex from which everything comes.

The Father works out of Love. The Son judges out of Love. Mary lives by Love. The angels sing out of Love. The Light exists because it is Love. The Song exists because it is Love. Life exists because it is Love. Oh, Love, Love, Love...! I annul myself in You. I rise again in You. I die as a human creature because You consume me. I am born as a spiritual creature because You create me.

Be blessed, blessed, blessed, Love, Third Person! Be blessed, blessed, blessed, Love, who are the love of the First Two! Be blessed, blessed, blessed, Love, who love the Two preceding you! Be blessed, You that love me. Be blessed by me, who love You because You allow me to love You and know You, O my Light...

After having written all of this, I looked for the previous contemplation of Paradise among the sheets. Why? Because I always distrust myself and wanted to see if there was a contradiction between the two. That would have convinced me that I am the victim of a deceit.

No. There is no contradiction. The present one is even clearer, but has the same essential lines. The preceding one is dated January 10, 1944. And since then I had never looked at it. I certify this as if on oath.

May 25th 1944: Jesus.
In the Evening

Jesus Says:

«In the Paradise which Love has had you contemplate there are only the 'living' Isaiah speaks about in the fourth chapter, one of the prophecies which will be read the Sunday after this one[38]. And the way to obtain this being 'alive' is stated by the following words. With the spirit of justice and with the spirit of charity already existing faults are canceled out, and one is protected against new forms of corruption[39].

This justice and this charity, which God gives you and which you must give Him, will lead you and keep you in the shadow of the eternal Tabernacle. There the heat of the passions and the darkness of the Enemy will become innocuous, for they will be neutralized by your Most Holy Protector, who, more loving than a hen with her brood, will keep you under the protection of his wings and defend you against every supernatural assault. But never separate yourselves from Him, who loves you.

Soul of mine, think of the Jerusalem which has been shown to you. Isn't it worth all care to possess it?

---

38   In the Missal in use in 1944.
39   Isaiah 4:4.

Overcome. I am awaiting you. We are awaiting you. Oh, these words, which We would like to say to all creatures, at least to all Christians, at least to all Catholics, and which we can say to so few!

That's enough, for you are weary. Rest, thinking of Paradise.»

June 29th 1944: Jesus.

Jesus Says

«Out of love for obedience and truth. You have been heavily punished for not having wanted to follow the inner 'voice' and the words of your Director. But if the punishment lasts, the sin has been annulled by the very cause that led you to offer resistance. You have acted for a loving reason, and love covers sin and destroys it. Do not do so any more, though. Above the voices of any kind is Mine and that of the one who speaks to you in My Name, and these should always be listened to. You have acted like a heedless child. But since I Am just, I calculate the attenuating circumstances and look at the loving reason which, even if human, is still love, and I shall be able to draw good even from this error of yours. Go in peace.»

Later Jesus Says:

«Every living being and everything about the living dies and vanishes, never to return. Joy, sorrow, health, illness, and life are episodes which come and dissolve, sooner or later, and do not come back, in that form, ever again. Joy or sorrow, health or illness may return in other forms and with other faces. But that specific joy, that specific sorrow, that illness, and that health never return. It is a thing of the moment. When that moment is over, another moment like it will come, but that one, never again.

And life... Oh, life, once over, never returns! You are given an hour of eternity, a moment of eternity, to conquer Eternity.

Have you never considered that this motif could be applied to the parable of the money Luke speaks about[40]?

You are given one coin of eternity. The Lord entrusts it to you and says, 'Go. Do business with your coin until I return.' And, on His return, or, rather, your return to Him, He asks you, 'What did you do with the coin you received?' And the faithful servant can happily respond, 'Here You are, my King. With this coin of eternity I did this work and that one and that other one. And, not by my calculation, but through the word of an angel, I know I have earned ten times as much.' And the Lord says to him, 'Well done, faithful servant! Since You have been faithful in a small matter, you shall have power over ten cities, and, in your case, you shall reign here, where I reign for eternity, at once, for you have worked as much as you could.'

---

40   Luke 19:11-27

Another, when called by God, will say, 'With your coin I did this and this. You see, my King, what is written about me.' And I shall say, 'Enter as well, for you have worked as much as you could.'

But to the one who says to Me, 'Here You are: the coin is just the same. I did not do business with it because I was afraid of your justice,' I shall say, 'Go and get to know Love in Purgatory and work there to conquer the kingdom, for you have been a slothful servant and did not take the trouble to get to know who I Am and judged Me to be unjust, doubting My justice and forgetting that I Am Love. Let your coin be turned into expiation.'

And to the one who presents himself to Me, saying, 'I squandered your coin and used it for my own enjoyment because I did not believe this Kingdom really existed and wanted to enjoy the hour which had been given me,' I shall say indignantly, 'Foolish and blaspheming servant! Let My gift be taken from you and deposited in the eternal Treasury, and as for you, go where God is not present and Life is not present, for you have wanted not to believe and have wanted to enjoy. You have enjoyed. You have already received, then, your joy of flesh without a soul. The Kingdom of eternity is forever closed to you.'

How often I would have to thunder these words if I were Justice alone! But Love is greater than my Justice. The former is perfect, and so is the latter. But Love is my nature and takes precedence over my other perfections. This is why I temporize with the sinner, working in such a way that the blameworthy one does not perish altogether.

I give you time. This is at once love and justice. What would you say if I struck you at the first mistake? You would say, 'Why, Lord! If You had given me time to reflect, I would have repented!' I leave you time. You are at fault one, two, ten, seventy times, and I could strike you. I give you time. So that you cannot say to Me, 'You did not show benignity'

No, it is you that are not benignant towards yourselves. And you defraud yourselves of the wealth which I have created for you. And you commit suicide, taking away the Life I have created for you.

Most of you waste or poorly use the coin of eternity which I give you, and you make the earthly day not, indeed, your eternal glory, but the means for eternal suffering. The minority, afraid of my Justice, remains motionless and condemns itself to learn who God as Love is amidst the flames of purgative love.

Only a very small portion is able to value My coin and invest it for a tenfold gain, plunge into love, like a fish into a clear fishpond, and go upstream to reach the source, its God, and say to Him, 'Here I am. I have believed, loved, and hoped in You. You have been my faith, my love, and my hope. I am now coming, and my faith and my hope are ceasing, and everything is becoming love. For I no longer need now to hope in You and in this Life. I now have You, my God. And loving You, just loving You, is the eternal task of this eternal Life of mine.'

Be one of these, soul of Mine, and My peace be with you to help you in this work.»

The Soul In Purgatory Of Montefalco

Extract from 'Who Dies Shall See...'
By Dolindo Ruotolo, Priest. Ch XIII

Before finishing the mystery and the absolute reality of Purgatory, we will speak of the manifestation of a soul in Purgatory, that happened in the town of Montefalco, in the Diocese of Spoleto, Italy, from September 2, 1918 to November 9, 1919. The following manifestations, with the evidence of witnesses, highly respected for their faith, had the confirmation of an ecclesial trial requested by Msgr. Peter Pacifici, Bishop of Spoleto, Italy from July 27 to August 8, 1921. Herewith is what happened.

All the extraordinary manifestations- 28 in total- happened in the Monastery of St.Leonard in Montefalco, where there lived a big Community of Poor Clares (The Poor Clares have their Monastery there to the present time)[41].

On September 2, 1918, the doorbell rang in the sacristy and Sister Marie Therese of Jesus, Abbess of the

---

41   The Poor Clares are cloistered Nuns, that is, they do not go outside their Monastery and hardly do they see anyone even when someone wants to communicate with them. The Nuns talk to people through a small grating. To accept donations the Nuns have a turning table through an opening in the door. Donations are put on the turning table and the Nun turns the table to pick up the donation

Monastery, went to answer it. A voice told her:

«I must leave here this alms.»

The Sister turned the rotating table and found 10 liras on it. The Abbess enquired after the reason for the money, whether it was for celebrating a special Mass for someone or for a Triduum or other prayers. The voice said:

«No reason.»

The Abbess asked: «Excuse me, but may I ask who are you?»

The voice said: «It is not important to know.»

The voice sounded kind, but sorrowful, far and in a hurry, like someone in hiding.

The same happened also on October 5, 1918, October 31, November 29, December 9, January 1 and 29, 1919, always in the same way; 10 liras left on the rotating table and to the Abbess' question, the voice answered:

«Prayer is always good.»

On March 14, 1919 when the Sisters were doing their examination of conscience, at about 8pm, the bell rang two times. The Abbess went to the door and upon turning the table she again found 10 liras. However nobody responded to her questions. Surprised, the Abbess called a servant girl and asked her to go around the outside of their Church that was closed at that hour of the day and only the Nuns kept the keys, to search if there was anybody outside. Nobody was around and nobody was in Church either. From then on the Sisters began to suspect that whoever was giving the alms was not an earthly person.

On April 11th , again like before, the 10 liras was found on the turning table, however this time the voice answered to the Abbess, asking for prayers for a deceased.

On May 2nd, occurred the 10th manifestation.

A little before the time of silence, about 9:30 pm, the doorbell rang again. This time the Abbess went with three other Sisters, Sister Mary Francis of the Five Wounds, Sister Amante Mary of St. Anthony and Sister Angelica Ruggeri. They found on the turning table 20 liras, in two of 10 liras notes, placed in the shape of a cross. Again nobody was in sight and nobody was in Church.

On May 25, June 4 and June 21 again 10 liras were found each time, on the turning table but nobody answered or was in sight.

On July 7, about 2 pm, the doorbell rang. The Abbess thought that there were children in Church and because the Nuns were doing their retreat, she chose not to answer. She closed her eyes to rest a bit but a voice outside the room said:

«The doorbell rang in the sacristy».

She then went to the Sacristy and she heard the usual voice that said: «I leave here 10 liras for the prayers».

«In the Name of God, who are you?» asked the Abbess.

The voice said: «It is not allowed » and no more words were heard.

The Abbess later asked the other Sisters if anyone of them had called her from the outside room. But nobody had called her.

On July 18, after the evening silence, about 9:30 pm, the Abbess went to close the door of the oven left open when the doorbell rang. She went to the sacristy and in saying the greeting: «Praised be Jesus and Mary», she heard the voice answering: «Amen», then it added: «I leave here the alms for the usual prayers». The Abbess, gathering her courage, asked: «In the name of God and the Holy Trinity, who are you?»

The same voice answered: «It is not allowed», and nothing else. Again nobody was around and the closed Church was empty.

On July 27, the Abbess found 10 liras on the turning table but she did not know who had put the alms there.

On August 12, about 8 pm, again the doorbell, again the 10 liras on the turning table. This time the Abbess had gone to the door with two other Nuns, Sister Mary Nazarena of the Sorrowful Mother and Sister Chiara Benedetta Josephine of the Sacred Heart. Again there was nobody in sight. The Reverend Father Alessandro Climati, Pastor of St Bartholomew's Church and Confessor of the Nuns was called in as well as Father Agazio Tabarrini, Pastor of Casale, Chaplain of the Monastery and Father Angelo, Guardian of the Franciscan Capuchins. They looked in the Church together with the servant girl. The Church was empty.

On August 19, about 6:30 pm, the doorbell rang again. The Abbess said the greeting «Praised be Jesus and Mary» and the voice answered: «Amen» and immediately said: «I leave this alms for the prayers». The Abbess answered: «We shall say the prayers, but keep your money and give it to someone who needs it more».

The voice in a sorrowful tone said: «Oh no, please take it, it is an act of mercy».

The Abbess asked: «Is it allowed to know who you are?» The voice answered: «It is always me» and nothing else was heard. 10 liras were left. The same happened on August 28 and September 4. The Abbess never got an answer. On September 16, about 9:15 pm the Abbess was locking the dormitory when she heard the doorbell ringing. She went to the door together with another Nun and they found 10 liras on the turning table. The Abbess decided not to take the money and was about to leave when she heard a voice saying: « Take it, it is to satisfy the Divine Justice». The Abbess said: «Repeat this short prayer: Be blessed the Holy, Most Pure, the Immaculate Conception, The most Holy Virgin Mary». The short prayer was faithfully repeated.

On September 21 on the turning table were found 10 liras but nobody was in sight. On October 3, about 9 pm, past the time of silence, the Abbess was looking out of her window in her room when she heard the doorbell. When the usual conversation took place, the Abbess refused to take the money saying that her Confessor was not pleased, because he thought that it was a diabolic manifestation. The answer came: «I am a soul in Purgatory. 40 years I have been in Purgatory because I squandered goods of the Church.»

On October 6, a Holy Mass was celebrated in suffrage of this soul. Shortly afterwards the doorbell rang and to the Abbess who went to the door, the voice said:

«Thank you very much. I leave here this alms.»

The Abbess wanted to talk some more but she received

no more answers. The sacristy was closed but on the turning table was left 10 liras. The same thing happened on October 10. When the Abbess asked more questions about its identity, the usual voice said: «The Judgment of God is right and just.»

«But how is it possible. I had several Masses said for you, and only one is enough to free a soul and you are still in Purgatory?»

The voice answered: «I receive only a small part of it.» The voice did not answer any other questions. Also this time were left 20 liras.

On October 20, at 8:45 pm, the time of silence had just started and the Abbess with Sister Mary Rosalia of the Cross and Sister Clare Giuseppa of the Sacred Heart were going upstairs when the doorbell rang. The Abbess found the usual 10 liras but no one answered. She did not take the alms and left to go to close the door of the dormitory. The doorbell rang again. She went again to the door and to her greeting: «Praised be Jesus and Mary», the voice said: «Amen». Then an almost inaudible the voice said: «Please take this alms, it is an act of mercy.» After the Abbess had taken it, the voice said: «Thank you!»

On Oct 30, at 2:45 pm, the Abbess heard a voice from the next room saying: «The doorbell rang». She went to open the grille of the door and to her usual greeting, the voice answered: «Amen. I leave here the alms.» The Abbess without letting it finish the words, immediately said: «Sorry, by the order of my Confessor I cannot take your alms. In the name of God and by the order of my Confessor, tell me who you are. Are you a Priest?

The voice answered: «Yes».

«Did the goods that you squandered belong to this Monastery?»

«No, but I have the permission to bring the money here», was the answer. The Abbess said: « From where did you take this money?»[42]

The soul said: «The Judgment of God is right and just.»

The Abbess said: «I do not believe that you are a soul, I believe you are someone who is making a poor joke.»

The soul said: «Do you want a sign?»

«No», the Abbess answered, «Because I am scared. I can go and call another Sister. I'll be right back.»

The soul said: «I cannot wait. I do not have the permission.»

Most likely it was not permitted to this soul to give a sign in the presence of others for the fear and bustle that would have followed.

The Abbess took the 10 liras and the soul said: «Now I enter the prayer.»

Up to that day the soul had put on the turning table 300 liras. When the soul thanked the Abbess for taking the money, the Abbess said: «Will you pray for me. For our Community and our Confessor?»

---

42   According to an inspiring suggestion of the English editor of the present book, Father Christopher Rengers, C.A.P.: «I was thinking too how this soul did get the money. My theory is that the priest had laid away bit by bit an unjust personal treasure. He had therefore been commanded to restore it little by little, just as he had accumulated it. So he was restoring the same identical coins he had unjustly hidden for private use later. It is just an imaginative theory and eliminates a need of other possible miracles.»

The soul answered: «Benedictus Dei qui...» (The blessing of God who..). The voice spoke softly going away till it could not be heard anymore. However the voice this time did not seem to be in as much a hurry as the previous times and was less hollow; whilst at other times it seemed to come from outside, now it seemed that it was talking into the right ear and when it left it was heard from the left ear.

On November 9 occurred the last of the manifestations. About 4:15 pm the Abbess from the dormitory heard the doorbell of the sacristy. At her greeting: «Praised be Jesus and Mary», the usual voice answered: « Be They praised forever. I thank you and all your Community because now I am out of all my suffering.» The Abbess replied: «Thank also the Priests who said many Masses for you, wouldn't you? The Confessor, Fr. Luigi Bianchi, Father Agazio?»

The voice said: «I thank you all.»

The Abbess remarked: «I would like to go to Purgatory where you were, in this way I would be more sure...»

The soul answered: «Do the Will of the Almighty».

The Abbess: «Will you pray for me, for the Community, for my parents if they are in Purgatory, for the Confessor, Fr. Luigi Bianchi, for the Pope, for the Bishops, for Cardinal Ascalesi?»

The soul said: «Yes».

The Abbess: «Bless me and the people I named».

The soul: « Benedictio Domini super vos». (The Blessing of God be on you all).

The morning before this last manifestation Fr Luigi

Bianchi S.J, celebrated a Holy Mass at the Privileged Altar in the Church of the Jesuits, the Church of Jesus in Rome.

At the beginning of the manifestations the voice of the deceased Priest was sad.

As time went by, it became more and more cheerful and the last time it sounded very happy. The sound of the doorbell initially was sad and feeble. It seemed now to convey a feeling of peace and cheerfulness in the heart of those who heard it. After the first manifestations, all the nuns were praying for the deceased as soon as they heard him. With the 300 liras that the soul brought, were celebrated 38 Masses for him.

This account is authentic, written by the Poor Clare Sisters of the Monastery of St. Leonard at Montefalco, Italy.

It was reported immediately to the Archbishop of Spoleto, Msgr. Pietro Pacifici, to His Eminence Cardinal Pompili, Vicar of the Holy Father in Rome, to His Eminence Cardinal Ascalesi in Naples, Italy and to many other persons. One of the 10 liras notes serial numbers 041161 and 2694 was kept in remembrance.

On July 1921, Msgr. Pietro Pacifici wanted to institute a canonical trial and he called Msgr. Giovanni Capobianco who was the Judge of the Court from Rome. The original acts of the trial are kept in the Archive of the Archbishop's Curia in Spoleto. They are 200 pages in protocol. In it is the deposition of twelve witnesses requested by the Postulator. These are seven Nuns, the Rev. Fr. Agazio Tabarrini, Chaplain of the Monastery, Franciscan Capuchin Fr. Valentino da Giano, Millei

Catherine, servant of the Monastery, Rev. Thomas Casciola, Associate Pastor at St. Bartholomew Church and Mr.Ponziani Vergari.

Three additional dispositions were added ex officio: the most Eminent Cardinal Alessio Ascalesi, Msgr. Climati and Dr. Alessandro Tassinari, medical doctor of Montefalco. In the appendix to the above, with other documents, are reported in the trial the acts of the first Investigation on the manifestations and the deposition of Fr. Luigi Bianchi SJ, certified by his Provincial because this Priest was unable to be present.

The result of the trial was positive hence the manifestations were juridical verified.

The sacristy in which the manifestations took place was made into a Chapel for the suffrages of the souls in Purgatory, especially of deceased Priests. It was blessed on February 25, 1924 and as of today, it is a centre of very ardent charity for the sufferings of the poor souls.

A Confraternity of the Souls in Purgatory was established, particularly the souls of Priests.

October 08th 1943: Final Repentance And Saving Mercy.

Jesus Says:

«My Mercy is so infinite that it works prodigies, whose power and form you will see only in the other life, to conquer the greatest number of souls for the Resurrection of the flesh in Christ.

I do not want you, marked with My Name, to die forever. I want to raise you up. I died to be able to raise you up. I squeezed my Blood out of My flesh like a bunch of pressed grapes so as to be able to raise you up. The drops of My Blood are in you and long to return to the Heart from which they have come.

I repeat what I said yesterday. There are few in whom My Blood does not give that minimum of merits - not through the fault of the Blood, but because of their response to It - capable of saving the soul. The Judases are not the mass, for often, after a vile life lived by a body in which the soul was kept a slave, a triumph of the soul over matter is obtained by the fact that in the final hour that soul, on the threshold of death, which frees the spirit from the flesh, turns to God, of whom it has conserved a memory, and takes refuge in Him.

And believe Me: in truth a throb of love, confidence, and repentance suffices to make the lavacre* of my merits descend upon the sinner and deliver him.

*referring to Baptism, the lavacre of spiritual regeneration.

My Justice is not yours, and my Mercy is very different from yours. When the number of those saved by my Love, all mercy, is seen, the virtues of the Lamb will be proclaimed with jubilant voices by all the spirits living in his Kingdom. For you are those saved by the Lamb who had Himself immolated for you. And if those who have always lived in Him and by Him, to the point of not knowing sensuality, will follow Him singing the canticle[43] known to them alone, those saved by His Mercy, at the final hour on earth, prostrated in loving adoration will bless Him eternally because He is a Saviour twice over for them. Saviour of Justice and Saviour of Love. By Justice He died to cleanse you in His Blood. By Love He gives you His Heart open to receive you while still sullied by sins and cleanse you in the fire of His love when, at death, you call Him, who loves you and promises you a Kingdom.»

---

43   Revelation 14, 1-5

October 09th 1943: The Continuity Of Life In God. 1 a.m.

Jesus Says:

«Do not grow sad, then, all of you that weep. Trust in Me and entrust to Me the destiny of your loved ones. Earthly time is short, children. I will soon call you where life lasts. So be holy to obtain eternal life, where your loved ones already await you or where they will reach you after purgation. The current separation is as short as an hour that quickly passes. Afterwards there comes the reunion of spirits in the Light and, in the future, the blessed resurrection, whereby you will rejoice not only in union with your loved ones, but also in the sight of those faces dear to you whose disappearance makes you weep if a theft had robbed you of the jewel dearest to you.

Nothing is changed, O children. Death does not separate you if you live in the Lord.

Those who have gone beyond earthly life are not separated from you. They cannot be, for they live in Me as you live. It is simply that, to offer you a human comparison, they have risen from the lower members to higher, more noble parts, and they thus love you more perfectly because they are even more united to Me and from Me draw perfection.

Only the damned are «dead.» They alone. But the others «live.»

They live, Maria. Understand: they live. Not cry. Pray. I will come soon.

The worker, as the evening falls, hastens his work to finish the task of his day and then go happily to rest after having received a worthy salary for it. When for a creature, too, the evening of life on earth falls, labour must be speeded up to give the finishing touches to the nearly completed work. And give them joyfully, considering that repose is near after so much fatigue and that the salary will be large because a lot of work was done.

I am a Master who remunerates well. I am a Father who waits for you to reward you. I am the one who loves you and has always loved you and will always love you. Not one of your tears is unknown to Me, and none will go unrewarded. Remain in Me more and more and do not fear. Do not be afraid that I will leave you alone. Even when I do not speak, I am with you.

You, alone? Oh, don't say that! You have your Jesus with you, and where Jesus is, all Paradise is. You are not alone. Mary was not alone in the little house in Nazareth. The angels surrounded her human solitude. You, Maria, are not alone. You have Me as a Father; you have Mary as a Mother; you have my saints as brothers and sisters and my angels as friends. Whoever lives in Me has everything, daughter.

I do not say to you, «Don't cry» I, too, cried[44], and so did Mary. But I say to you, «Don't cry with those human

---

44   I cried, as in the death of Lazarus in John 11, 35.

tears which are a negation of faith and hope. Never cry these. Have faith not only in the great realities of Faith, but also in my secret words. They are mine; be certain of this. And have hope in my promises. When I come to give you Life, you will see that you have not lost those you have wept for. Those who die without Jesus in their hearts are lost.

As for you, remain in Jesus. In Him you will find all you long for.

I will dry every tear from your eyes forever just as I now console every sorrow of yours, which I cannot free you from because it is of use for the glory of your God and your own. «The winter[45] of life quickly passes, my dove, and when the eternal spring comes, I will come to crown you with flowers, taking away the thorns which you bore out of love for Me.»

---

45   Winter ... is a picture taken from the Song of Songs 2: 10-14.

October 09th 1943: The Common Destiny And Special Service.

At the End of the Morning and After My Tremendous Crisis and Communion.

Jesus Says:

«There are the ones who come to Me by a common destiny and there are the ones predestined to be something special in my service.

Among the predestined there are those who lived like angels from birth on, and there are those who became angels, out of love, after having been men. But they are equally those predestined to be stars illuminating the way for their brothers and sisters who are going and who need so many lights to go.

I am Light. Most powerful Light. And I ought to be enough to guide the peoples on the road leading to Heaven. But men, whose eyes are bending down excessively towards the mire, no longer bear the absolute Light. They can no longer receive it because in them there is lacking the spiritual exercise of the mind turned to God and confidence in God. The poor men either are separated from Me and do not look at Me because they do not think of Me, or they are crushed by their superficial mentality, which brings God to be seen and thought of in terms of their own measure. Therefore, not humbly, but only wretchedly, say, «I am too different from the way God wants man to be and cannot raise my eyes to God.»

Oh, blind men and fools! Is it the healthy who go to the doctor? Is it the rich who go to the benefactor? No. It is the sick and the poor that resort to whoever can help them. And you are the poor and the sick, and I am your Lord and Doctor.

I say it to no avail. You are afraid of Me. You are not afraid of sinning and wedding Satan, but you are afraid to look at Me and come close to Me.

And then, so that you will not die outside my Way, I give you the stars with a gentle light which are nothing but emanations of Me, part of Me which comes to you in such fashion that it does not induce foolish terror in you. I - the eternal Sun - penetrate my predestined ones with Myself, and these radiate my Light in your midst and give forth currents of spiritual attraction to draw you to Me, who await you on the threshold of the heavens.

Woe to the earth if a day were to come when God's eye could no longer choose from among the children of man the beings predestined to be my bearers of the Light and the Voice! Woe! It would mean that among billions of men there is no longer a just or generous one, for the predestined are among the just who never offended Justice and the generous who have overcome everything, beginning with themselves, to serve Me.

You are among the latter, little creature who live by love. You are among these. After so much torment you understood that only I could be for you what your soul wanted, and you came. But I had chosen you before you existed to be the voice of the Voice of Jesus the Master. I have waited for this hour, Maria, with the heart of a father and spouse; I have followed you with My gaze, patiently awaiting the hour to tell you My Will and My Word. Nothing was hidden from Me about what you would do that was less good, but neither was anything hidden about what you would dare to do from the moment you would hurl yourself into the current of love.

You will say, «You revealed Yourself so late, O Lord.» Late. I would have wanted it to be much sooner, daughter, but I had to work you as the goldsmith does with rough gold.

I shaped you twice. In your mother's womb to give you to the world, but later, within Me to give you to Heaven and make you a bearer of my Light into the world. I knew when you would come and when you would be mature for service. God is not in a hurry, for God knows everything about the lives of his children.

The hour has come in which you are no longer a woman, but just a soul of your Lord, an instrument, you said. And when you wrote[46] that, you did not know that My love would use you in this way after so many years of trial. Now go, act, and speak according to My desire. I do not say «command.» I say «desire,» for one commands a subordinate and one makes a request of a friend, and you are My friend.

And don't be afraid. Of anything or anyone. Neither the forces of the earth nor the forces of hell will be able to harm you, for you are with Me. What you say is not your word; it is My word, which I place on your lips so that you will repeat it to the deaf of the earth. What you do is My power, which I give you for the good of those dying in

---

[46] see the Autobiography of Maria Valtorta

spiritual starvation.

You are not the poor Maria, a weak woman, sick, alone, unknown, subject to treachery. You are My beloved disciple, and I swear to you that even if the whole world moved to wage war on you, it could not take away from you what I have given you, for I am with you.

You have understood clearly. The north[47], the peoples who now invade or try to invade the Christian land par excellence- the one where Rome is, the seat of my Church. A punishment merited by the embezzlers, who have bowed their heads, previously marked with my sign, before the idols of the lying foreign powers that are now the first to bring torment.

A sorrow for the honest is this hour. But not willed by Me. Make the sorrow come to have a limit. Do so by returning to Me.

If the four powers of the north were to ally themselves against you in a horrid conspiracy of dark forces, the light would fade out on your soil, and the blood of the martyrs would again become fresh from new blood dripping upon it.

There must be very, very much prayer, daughter of My love. I can no longer ask you for other sacrifices of affections because you are naked like Me on the cross. But if it were possible, I would ask you for many others for this purpose. I will help you; but, since I need tears for holy water upon Italy, bespattered with mire, I advise you that I will render your affliction harsh so that it will avail for many losses and for many acts of forgiveness by God regarding Italy.

---

47   as it is said in Jeremiah 1: 14-16

Say with Me, «Lord, to preserve Italy from new catastrophes, and especially from those of the spirit, I agree to drink the chalice of pain. Remain with me, Lord, as I consummate my Passion as a little redeemer,» and I will always remain with you until it is time to take you there, where the Passion ceases and the glorious resurrection in Me begins.»

———

www.ingramcontent.com/pod-product-compliance
Lightning Source LLC
Chambersburg PA
CBHW070623050426
42450CB00011B/3116